THE CANCER MISFIT

THE CANCER MISFIT

A GUIDE TO NAVIGATING LIFE AFTER TREATMENT

SASKIA LIGHTSTAR

HAY HOUSE

Carlsbad, California • New York City
London • Sydney • New Delhi

Published in the United Kingdom by:
Hay House UK Ltd, The Sixth Floor, Watson House,
54 Baker Street, London W1U 7BU
Tel: +44 (0)20 3927 7290; Fax: +44 (0)20 3927 7291; www.hayhouse.co.uk

Published in the United States of America by:
Hay House Inc., PO Box 5100, Carlsbad, CA 92018-5100
Tel: (1) 760 431 7695 or (800) 654 5126
Fax: (1) 760 431 6948 or (800) 650 5115; www.hayhouse.com

Published in Australia by:
Hay House Australia Pty Ltd, 18/36 Ralph St, Alexandria NSW 2015
Tel: (61) 2 9669 4299; Fax: (61) 2 9669 4144; www.hayhouse.com.au

Published in India by:
Hay House Publishers India, Muskaan Complex,
Plot No.3, B-2, Vasant Kunj, New Delhi 110 070
Tel: (91) 11 4176 1620; Fax: (91) 11 4176 1630; www.hayhouse.co.in

A catalogue record for this book is available from the British Library.

Tradepaper ISBN: 978-1-40196-041-4
E-book ISBN: 978-1-78817-403-9
Audiobook ISBN: 978-1-78817-594-4

Interior illustrations: Jade Ho Designs

Printed in the United States of America.

Dedicated to all the survivors out there who
struggle with life after cancer treatment.

Contents

List of Exercises

Introduction:
Where the Journey Really Begins

Those of us who have been through cancer know that surviving treatment isn't where the journey ends. In fact, for many of us, this is where the hardest part of the cancer journey begins.

When we're first diagnosed, we have no choice but to do whatever we have to not to die. Everything we are just stops, and our focus becomes cancer and only cancer. And then, if we're one of the lucky ones, we survive the treatment and it's time to get on with our lives. For some, this transition is an easy one; they manage to slip back into their old lives with ease and put the whole experience of treatment behind them. Others are so overjoyed the treatment is over that they move on with a spring in their step, excited about everything that lies ahead.

And then there's the rest of us. The ones who don't find it so easy and simple to move on from the treatment and trauma of cancer, the ones who feel we've been left in limbo, stuck in a no-man's land between who we used to be and who we are today. We try to 'go back to normal' once the treatment is finished, only to discover there's no normal to go back to. We're unfamiliar with the person we are now, and everything around us feels strange and different.

There's loads of advice and support available for when you're first diagnosed with cancer. There's also a whole load of resources, including a vast range of literature, for when you go through treatment. But, after that, the support just seems to stop, as though it's assumed that survivors will just slip back into normality as if nothing has happened. But I think this is the most important time of all – the time when we piece our lives back together.

Life *after* cancer treatment was the hardest part of the journey for me. Suddenly, the support dissipated: doctors had newly diagnosed patients to focus on, and my family and friends believed I was through the worst of it and got on with their lives, assuming it would be as easy for me to do the same. But, in truth, it felt as though I'd just been hit by a freight train. I was dazed and confused, standing at the beginning of a new chapter of my life with utterly no idea what had just happened, who I now was or what I was supposed to do next.

And I believe there are many other survivors out there who feel this way.

Forty per cent of people who've experienced cancer report feeling anxious or depressed following the completion of treatment.* And that's just the people who are willing to admit it. Many survivors feel a sense of guilt and shame about struggling with

---

* Inhestern, L., Beierlein, V., Bultmann, J. C., et al. (19 May 2017), 'Anxiety and depression in working-age cancer survivors: a register-based study', *BMC Cancer*, 17 (article number 347)

life after making it through treatment. Many don't talk about how hard they find life after cancer treatment, because they believe they're supposed to be happy now. They don't speak out about how they're really feeling, because everything has already revolved around them for too long. So, they just keep their mouths shut and struggle in silence.

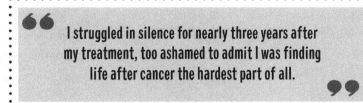

I struggled in silence for nearly three years after my treatment, too ashamed to admit I was finding life after cancer the hardest part of all.

I didn't want to be a burden to anyone, I didn't want to make it all about me any more. I felt I couldn't ask for more support and attention from friends and family after they'd already made the world revolve around me for so long during chemo, radiation, reconstruction and so on. And in any case, how could I possibly complain after I'd survived cancer treatment, when hundreds of thousands of people weren't as lucky?

So, I just kept quiet and battled with all the feelings of fear, depression, guilt, and so on, alone – until it got so bad, I became determined to find a way to be happy again. And through that determination, I didn't just become happy again, I became the happiest I've ever been in my life. My journey was one of painful but profound and necessary transformation; a journey of self-discovery and self-healing. I tried anything and everything that would help me to find a life of peace and joy after going through treatment. And through that self-healing and inner work, I managed not only to overcome the trauma and struggle of my cancer journey, but to let go of all the struggles and issues that I had suffered from my whole life – things like insecurity, anxiety and fear. I managed to overcome all of these things and find a happiness that comes from deep within; a happiness that no person, place or thing – not even cancer – can ever take away from me.

This book shares with you the path I took to living the greatest chapter of my life. It will help you to let go of what was and to embrace what is and what will be. It will help you to accept and understand that during the cancer treatment journey, when you were focused on staying alive, a beautiful transformation was taking place deep within you. This book will introduce you to the person you have become and show you the way to find a new life; a life that is full of confidence, happiness and peace.

You don't have to go through the darkness, because I already did – and now I'm giving you the knowledge and hindsight from my experience so that, even after cancer treatment, you can live the greatest chapter of *your* life, too.

Who is this book for?

The Cancer Misfit is for survivors who feel confused, misunderstood, isolated, overwhelmed, fearful or anxious after treatment. It is a life raft for survivors who have finished cancer treatment – whether that was last week, last month, last year or ten years ago – and are struggling with what comes next. It is a guidebook to living your best life, even after going through cancer treatment, and even if you still have cancer.

It doesn't matter whether you are male or female, it doesn't matter what kind of cancer you've had and it doesn't matter whether you are in remission or still have the disease: the same feelings and thoughts still apply.

The Cancer Misfit is for:

➡ survivors suffering a loss of identity after treatment, who don't understand why they don't feel like their old selves any more

➡ survivors suffering from insecurity, depression or low self-worth

➡ survivors who find themselves suddenly reassessing their lives, questioning what they're doing and what it is they really want

➡ survivors who are overwhelmed with fear and anxiety about the cancer coming back – or, for those living with cancer, the day-to-day reality of this

➡ survivors struggling to deal with the physical, mental and emotional after-effects of treatment or with the side-effects of medication

➡ survivors struggling in silence, feeling too guilty to speak out because they believe they should just be grateful that they're still here

➡ survivors who allow cancer to define everything they are

If you've been through cancer treatment and are now cancer-free but still struggling to move on, this book is for you.

If you've been through cancer treatment and haven't yet been given the all-clear; or if you're still living with cancer and possibly will be for the rest of your life, this book is also for you.

If you're currently undergoing treatment and want to prepare yourself for what comes next, for what lies ahead of you – to make sure you have the wisdom and support you need for the next chapter after treatment – this book is for you, too.

The words in these pages are the steps of a ladder that will slowly but surely get you out of the darkness of cancer and into the light, where you truly belong.

Why the 'Cancer Misfit'?

I don't think we should be called survivors for ever, because it sounds like we're in some perpetual struggle. I don't know about you, but I don't want to always feel like I'm just 'surviving'; I want to feel like I'm living my greatest life.

That's why I came up with the term 'cancer misfit'. Cancer misfits are those who survived cancer treatment and now don't quite fit into the neat round hole we used to. And that's OK. You don't need to fit into any round holes any more – or into any square or triangular holes, either. You don't need to fit into a pretty package or be the same as everybody else. You just need to accept and love yourself exactly as you are. You are not cancer. You are not broken. You are not fear. You are not the negative talk you hear in your head. You are not 'less than'.

And, most importantly, you are not, and will never be, alone. There are millions of us all over the world and we stand united with you. We are the crazy, cool cancer misfits trying to find our way after the terrible trauma of treatment. We are everywhere. We are a tribe without even knowing it. After my treatment finished, I felt as though I didn't belong anywhere. I felt isolated and alone. But now I realize I have all of you, you have me, and we all have each other. We are the cancer misfits and we get it, when no one else does. The people around you might not understand, but I do. I get you, and you get me.

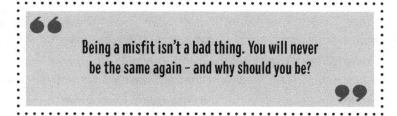

Being a misfit isn't a bad thing. You will never be the same again – and why should you be?

You went through treatment and made it to the other side: own that and be proud – and stop trying to fit into the life you once lived. You're so much bigger and more extraordinary now than that person you remember being before being diagnosed. You might feel as though you don't fit in, but you fit in with me perfectly. You might feel different from how you were before, but you're exactly the same as me. So, welcome to the gang, and rest assured that you need never feel alone again.

Who am I, and why should you trust me?

I was all rock 'n' roll before I got cancer. I lived a big, brash and beautiful life. I was the one dancing on the bar, instigating mischief and handing out shots of absinthe. That was me on a typical Saturday night (before being bulldozed by a cancer diagnosis). But by the time I reached the other side of treatment, I wasn't that person any more. I wasn't the person I'd been when I'd first received my diagnosis. I had changed fundamentally. The problem was that I didn't know this at first; I finished treatment and assumed my life would go back to the way it was. Only it never did. I kept waiting, kept hoping, and kept searching for my old life, for the person I used to be, but she never came back. And that was my problem; that was why I suffered for so long after treatment, continuing to feel confused, lost and alone. I was too busy looking for the old me, too busy longing for what was. It felt as though there once was this girl who got diagnosed with cancer, she survived the treatment – and suddenly that girl wasn't there any more. Instead I was this new person that I didn't recognize, a new me who I'd never met before in my life. The person I'd known intimately for more than 40 years had gone, and been replaced by a stranger.

That's when the pain began for me. That's when the bewilderment and loss swallowed me up in one big gulp. At the time, it felt as though I'd never move on from the treatment and from the loss of who I used to be. But through the journey I made, I came to realize how wrong I was. Cancer gave me the kick up the ass that I needed in order to reassess my whole life. In order to be as happy as I am today (and, truthfully, I am ridiculously happy), I needed to look within and learn how to truly connect with myself in order to uncover who I really am (and always have been) deep inside. Cancer led me to explore all things mind, body and spirit, and as a consequence I transformed into a version of myself I would never, in a million years, have imagined that I could be.

I'm not trying to convince you that cancer is the best thing that ever happened to you, but it doesn't have to be the worst thing that ever happened to you, either. Contrary to what you may currently believe, cancer hasn't stolen your life, who you are, your beauty, your confidence or anything else. Cancer has just changed you, and you need to take the time to get to know who you have become as a consequence of those changes.

I learned the hard way that you need to go through the process of saying goodbye to your former self and to get to know the person you've become. By doing so, you'll realize that you've in fact transformed into someone even more beautiful as a consequence of the ordeal that you went through and survived.

The moment I realized I wasn't the same person that I remembered from before the cancer, was the moment I set myself free. The chains of sadness and loss, my resentment of the disease, and my constant dwelling on what had been before cancer – that all just faded away as I looked in the mirror and met the new me for the very first time. It was like a rebirth; the most wonderful opportunity to start all over again. And now I want to offer that same incredible opportunity to you.

Spiritual mumbo jumbo

Having a serious, life-threatening illness like cancer has a huge impact on the way you look at life for ever. It can make you question things you never even thought about before, like the meaning of everything: who am I? What am I doing here? Why is life so hard? Why did I get cancer? Many survivors say that, after being diagnosed, they started exploring the idea of a spiritual path because they wanted answers, solutions and to find the way to live a truly happier and more meaningful life. Cancer was my introduction to spirituality, too. It was the catalyst that made me decide to look within and bring more peace to my life.

Of course, spirituality means different things to different people. That's why I love it so much – because it can mean whatever you want it to. To some, spirituality is closely tied to their religion or the path of their particular faith. To others, spirituality is simply the relationship they have with themselves. For others still, spirituality is about having a holistic approach to life or about their connection to nature or to art and creativity.

For me, spirituality is about believing in a power greater than myself and knowing that when I allow that power to enter my life and guide me, my life becomes pretty damn amazing.

> 'The spiritual path... is simply the journey of living our lives. Everyone is on a spiritual path; most people just don't know it.'
>
> MARIANNE WILLIAMSON, *A RETURN TO LOVE*

Initially I was terrified of what people would think of me if they knew I'd started meditating and saying positive affirmations to myself out loud in the mirror. But then I realized it wasn't anyone else's business. This was about me. I was doing this for myself, to heal myself after the hell of cancer treatment.

I'm not saying that once you engage with spirituality you'll never struggle, or have any negative feelings again, but just as healthy eating and regular exercise protect and nurture the body, mindfulness and spirituality protect and nurture your heart, your mind and your soul. So that's why you'll find me talking a lot of spiritual mumbo jumbo in this book – because, quite simply, I know it works. Spirituality has completely transformed the way I feel about myself; it's given me the strength and tools to handle fear, anxiety and all other kinds of negative emotions.

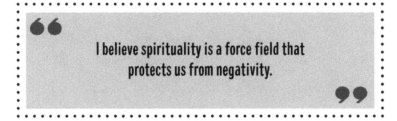

I believe spirituality is a force field that protects us from negativity.

So, if you are new to spirituality then just go gently; keep an open mind and an open heart. I'll be offering you a selection of spiritual ideas and tools; take what connects and resonates with you and leave the parts that don't. Just have the willingness to give each suggestion a shot, because it may turn out to be just what you need to let go of your experience of cancer treatment and to truly move on with your life, to a happiness you may have all but given up on.

What I need from you

Before we embark on this journey together, I'm going to ask you to make a commitment to yourself, here and now. Below is a loving contract between you and yourself in which you'll commit to turning the next page, to going forward on this journey of self-discovery, in order to be truly happy.

So, are you ready?

If so, please read the agreement below and sign on the dotted line, so you can begin this incredible, life-changing journey.

⇨ A COMMITMENT TO MYSELF ⇦

I, ..., hereby agree to commit myself to making the journey that will bring the joy, confidence and peace that I so rightfully deserve.

I will do my very best to keep an open mind, to have the willingness to try new things and to see myself and the world from a different perspective.

I agree to try all of the exercises offered to me, no matter how silly some of them are, because if I don't, then I'll never know whether they'll work for me or not. I'll remember not to take myself too seriously, and just to have fun with this journey.

I won't put pressure on myself, because I know that doing my best is enough and perfection isn't needed here.

I will believe in my heart that I am worthy of moving on after cancer treatment and of discovering a kind of happiness I never knew existed.

I commit to believing I can transform my life from the inside out and can become the happiest person I know.

I believe I can do this and, most of all, I know I deserve it.

Signed on this day, ... (date),

by .... (signature).

Cancer Is So Limited (extract)

...cancer is so limited –

It cannot cripple love.

It cannot shatter hope.

It cannot corrode faith.

It cannot eat away peace.

It cannot destroy confidence.

It cannot kill friendship.

It cannot shut out memories.

It cannot silence courage.

It cannot invade the soul.

It cannot reduce eternal life.

It cannot quench the spirit.

It cannot cancel resurrection.

ROBERT L. LYNN

I Survived. What Now?

The treatment is over, so why don't you have a big smile on your face and a spring in your step? Because the hardest part of the cancer journey sometimes comes after treatment, when you're left to fend for yourself, expected to just slip back neatly into your life where you left off, before cancer got in the way.

This is the time when you feel the most vulnerable and unsupported. Previously, everything revolved around you and your cancer, then suddenly it all stopped and you're on your own, trying to cope with all the feelings that come up now that the nightmare of treatment is over. This is the time when everything hits you; when the enormity of what you just went through punches you right in the face and knocks you over, and you're left lying on the floor, feeling completely winded, bewildered and afraid.

> The treatment wasn't the dark time for me; it was afterwards, when I fell into a black hole.

I've seen a lot of Instagram and Facebook posts showing people celebrating their last chemotherapy; of their happy smiles and bald heads, rejoicing that their cancer treatment is finally over. But I never had a moment like that. There was no finality for me, no moment when I thought to myself, *Phew, the worst is over.* I didn't heave a sigh of relief, because in truth I felt no relief at all. I felt daunted and overwhelmed. My life had revolved around cancer for so long, and now that the illness was over, I felt like I'd just been left in a vast open space where cancer treatment used to be, and I had no idea what to do with that. Was I really supposed to just pick up where I'd left off? Just press rewind on the video-recorder-of-life to the me I was before cancer, and get on with it? I tried to but it just didn't work. The life I remembered just didn't fit any more. Everything felt different: I felt different, life felt different, the whole world felt different.

I want you to know that you are not expected to just pick up from where you left off, from before you were diagnosed, and that there is no need to panic if you don't snap back to normal once the treatment is over. Everything you're feeling is part of the whole cancer journey. The biggest mistake we make is to assume that the journey is over just because the treatment is. The reality is that your journey with cancer is far from over, because life *after* treatment is the most transformational part of all.

One of my biggest mistakes was to believe there was something wrong with me because I struggled to move on with my life. But it's perfectly normal to feel confused, lost and broken after treatment, and you can rest assured that the more confused, lost and broken you are feeling right now, the more certain you can be that you're in the process of a big transformation and that something wonderful is beginning to happen.

Stop beating yourself up

Often, cancer survivors are too hard on themselves for not transitioning back quickly enough into everyday life, after treatment has finished. Friends and family may expect you to bounce back immediately; to be grateful you're still alive and to simply dive into a new chapter. And that assumption can put even more pressure on you to 'snap out of it' and to pretend you're jumping for joy, when in fact you're feeling the opposite.

The truth is that cancer treatment is a very serious trauma and it takes time to recover. It can take months for the poison of chemotherapy to leave your body, and it can take months for you to heal emotionally, mentally and spiritually from the suffering you've endured.

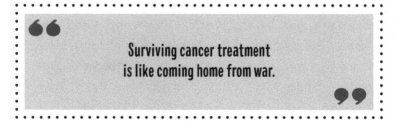

> **Surviving cancer treatment
> is like coming home from war.**

If a soldier were serving a tour of duty in a place of extreme conflict, would you expect them to return home and immediately be full of joy because they made it back alive? No, because they'd have been through hell; they'd have experienced serious trauma, and that changes a person for ever.

Cancer is no different, and you are no different. You also went to war, you also fought a battle, you also returned to 'reality' shell-shocked and changed by the trauma you went through. And just like those soldiers who return from a tour of duty, you'll never be the same again and you need time to recover. The battle took a toll on your mind, your body and your soul, so now you need to give yourself the time, love and compassion necessary in order to truly heal and move on.

If you ignore how you're really feeling, if you try to put on a brave face to keep friends and family happy, you'll stay stuck where you are. The pain you're carrying will continue to weigh heavy on your shoulders and you'll struggle to truly recover. But if you accept where you are and how you're feeling right now, and you use the exercises and tools I offer you, you can – and you will – move on and find true happiness.

Before, you were so focused on staying alive, on doctor's appointments and your treatment, that you didn't have a chance to really comprehend what was going on, to really pause for a moment and just feel the feelings and think the thoughts. But now that the treatment is over, all those thoughts and feelings you pushed down and ignored (because you had more important things to focus on, like not dying) have all come rushing up to the surface like a giant tsunami.

This happened to me and I just couldn't understand what was going on. I had survived cancer treatment, my hair was finally growing back, I had eyelashes and eyebrows again, and I was beginning to lose the weight I'd gained due to the steroids I was given during chemo. This was all good stuff – it was bloody great stuff – but I still wasn't jumping up and down with glee and gratitude. I thought it was depression, but in fact I was still processing the trauma of what I'd been through. For some people that takes a matter of weeks or months, but for me it took years. The good news is that it won't take you that long because I have condensed those years of learning and exploring into this book so that you can move on, and live your happiest chapter so far, as soon as possible.

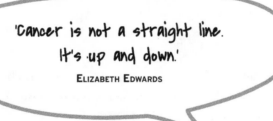

'Cancer is not a straight line. It's up and down.'

ELIZABETH EDWARDS

I want to give you the peace of mind that whatever you are feeling right now is absolutely OK and perfectly normal. There is no reason to feel guilt and shame because you survived but are struggling to be happy about it. The way you are feeling right now is not wrong or bad; there is no wrong or bad on your journey after cancer treatment. You're putting way too much pressure on yourself if you think you can snap your fingers and magically mould yourself back into your old life.

Just know this: if *I* could find my way out of the black hole I fell into after cancer treatment, if *I* could find my way to confidence, happiness and peace, then so can you.

The cancer cliff

When the cancer treatment stops, suddenly you go from being surrounded by people helping and supporting you to being back in the big wide world and fending for yourself. So, of course, this can be a daunting time. The support you had throughout treatment felt safe and nurturing, like you were being protected. But now, all of a sudden, that safety net has gone, and it can feel as though you're about to free-fall, with no one there to catch you. It's like you're standing on the edge of a cliff, about to jump into the unknown.

That is the cancer cliff.

It's the cliff from where you look at the long drop between your experience with cancer treatment and the daunting prospect of what comes next.

Sometimes it's not as simple as just turning the page and going from one chapter of our lives straight into another. Sometimes we have to sit in that uncomfortable place in between. Sometimes, in order to move on from one chapter to the next, we have to accept that there's going to be an uncomfortable period of transition, a time of not knowing – and that isn't a pleasant place to be. Nobody likes being in limbo; nobody likes standing on the edge of the cliff staring down at a vast empty space, not knowing what's to come. But this time is vital for you to process what you've been through, so that you don't hold on to the ordeal and trauma and take it with you into the future.

Right now, you're stuck in a place that's no longer cancer treatment, but it's not moving on after cancer treatment, either. You're at the edge of the cancer cliff. You're feeling daunted, scared to take a leap of faith and truly let go so that you can move on. You're trying to let go of something that has become familiar and normal to you, and it's hard to let go when you're not too sure what you're supposed to hold on to next.

It's a scary time right now, but it won't last for ever. The in-between feeling will pass. You just need to understand what is happening to you.

I spent nearly three years standing at the edge of the cancer cliff, too scared to jump. I was too afraid to take the plunge, to let go of who I used to be and to soar towards who I had become. That's why I wrote this book – to give you the wings you need so you can feel truly safe about stepping off the edge of what you know to reach the new life you deserve.

> 'We have to continually be jumping off cliffs and developing our wings on the way down.'
> **KURT VONNEGUT**

Remember that those who don't dare to jump never truly learn to fly. You have to learn to get comfortable with being uncomfortable, to know it's OK to be in a place of in between and of not knowing. It just means you're in-between an old chapter and a new one.

No normal to go back to

'Go back to normal.' There should be a rule that no one is allowed to say those four words to anyone who has gone through cancer treatment. How can we go back *anywhere* after going through cancer? Trying to 'go back to normal' is a waste of time; it's impossible because there is no normal to go back to. The life we knew before cancer has gone, and as long as we keep trying to go back to it, we will continue to carry our cancer experience with us wherever we go.

So how about you just stop trying to go back? If you're focused on the past, on how and who you used to be, then you can't see the person you've become, the transformed person you are today. When I kept trying to get back to the old me, I would keep failing because the cancer treatment had made me a completely different person. But I didn't know that; I had no one to tell me what I'm explaining to you right now, so I wasted nearly three years banging my head on a brick wall and all I did was cause myself a whole lot of pain.

Please don't try to 'go back to normal' after the trauma of cancer treatment, because you will not find it. The normal you remember before the treatment has gone, and the sooner you make peace with that, the sooner you can truly move on. The sooner you can accept that you have transformed into a whole new, beautiful person, the sooner your new life of happiness and peace can begin.

'We can't go back to who we once were. We can only go on and become the person we were meant to be.'
ANTHONY T. HINCKS, *AN AUTHOR OF LIFE, VOL. 1*

It's time to stop trying to go back so you can start to truly move forward. This may sound daunting, but I will show you the way to let go of the old and welcome the new. You are a new, improved version of yourself now; so much stronger and more beautiful, you just don't realize it yet... but you will.

You can do this.

CHAPTER 2

Where Have I Gone?

The moment I was told I had cancer – that very millisecond – something in me switched and I went straight into 'survival mode'. It's what we do when we're hit right between the eyes with something devastating: our body, our mind, our soul, every fibre of our being goes into shock and our survival instinct immediately kicks in. In that instant, everything else in my life faded away; all I could focus on was the fact that I had cancer and I had to do everything within my power to make sure I didn't die. Every cell, vein, pore, thought and breath zoned in on one thing and one thing only: staying alive.

My survival mode switched on and everything else switched off. I remember the long chemo needles, the radiation, the mastectomy, my hair falling out, the gruelling rehabilitation after all my lymph nodes were removed. But I don't remember feeling any despair or self-pity while going through it all. It was what it was. I didn't have a choice; the only alternative was to let the cancer kill me, and obviously that wasn't an option. I was doing what had to be done – I was doing what millions of other people had to do – and I just got on with it.

Survival mode is a natural instinct. When a bear is chasing you, you don't pause to reflect on the situation and figure out how you feel about it. No – you run for your life. Being told you have cancer is much the same. You instinctively switch to survival mode and do whatever you have to do to make sure you don't die.

When my doctor told me I had stage-three breast cancer, I would have shattered into a million little pieces on the floor if that survival mode hadn't kicked in. Instead, it was as though I became completely numb. I went through the experience of treatment but somehow it never managed to really penetrate my soul. It stayed on the surface. My beautiful long curls fell out, my breast was cut off, my body became bloated from the steroids, but inside I somehow felt nothing. And it was this numbness that allowed me to get through it all.

But here's the thing: even though we are numb, even though we are 100 per cent zoned in on the cancer treatment and staying alive, there's a huge transformation taking place within us, of which we're completely unaware. And I call that process the cancer cocoon.

The cancer cocoon

Some people believe a cocoon is a resting place, but it's far from that. Inside a cocoon there is much happening; much work and evolution, transformation and regeneration. And similarly, during our cancer treatment something within us has been hard at work.

While we were having treatment, we had tunnel vision. We were too busy trying to survive the cancer to notice the magical metamorphosis going on inside us. A true miracle was taking place while we were meeting the prospect of death face to face. We were metamorphosing into somebody new; remoulding, realigning and readjusting, to re-emerge as a newer version of ourselves. Just as a caterpillar does when it transforms into a butterfly.

'Keep up your faith to go high and fly, even after so many pains and sorrow. You can turn from a caterpillar to a butterfly. Life gives you a second chance: a call to grow.'

ANA CLAUDIA ANTUNES,
THE TAO OF PHYSICAL AND SPIRITUAL

This is the secret: while you were going through the pain and sorrow of cancer treatment, everything inside you was dissolving and evolving, letting go of old parts of yourself and creating new ones. A whole new you was starting to take form.

The problem is that if you don't know a transformation has taken place, then you interpret it as the loss of your old self, as though the cancer stole who you are, when you have simply changed from a caterpillar into a butterfly. So yes, you could say cancer treatment took part of you away, but in doing so it allowed a purer part of who you are to come to the surface.

Fear Of Moving On

FOMO usually stands for the Fear of Missing Out; the anxiety that an exciting or interesting event may currently be happening that you are not part of. But FOMO, for a cancer survivor, means the Fear Of Moving On – the anxiety of letting go of your old life and of who you used to be before the cancer diagnosis.

After treatment, I was too dazed and confused to recognize the process I was going through – I hadn't a clue about the concept of the cancer cocoon – and so I just refused to let go of the old me. I clung on to the memories of her, longing to go back. I was living in the past, completely oblivious to the present, unaware there was any beauty to be found in the now. I wanted my hair back. I wanted my body back. I wanted the old me back, and I wanted it back just the way it was before I got cancer.

But that longing was futile. All I was doing was torturing myself, because that old me wasn't me any more.

That me was gone.

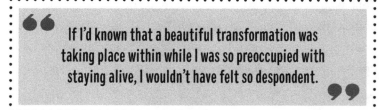

> **If I'd known that a beautiful transformation was taking place within while I was so preoccupied with staying alive, I wouldn't have felt so despondent.**

I wouldn't have tried so hard to get the old me back. If I had understood, I would have been more willing to get to know the person I had transformed into and I would have welcomed her with loving open arms. But instead I wasted nearly three years of my life trying to get back the old me, who just wasn't there any more. Please don't do that to yourself; don't look back. Nothing positive will come of it, and you will never find happiness for yourself down that road, I can promise you.

The cancer treatment is over, and a lot of what and who you were before the cancer has gone with it. No amount of yearning or praying is going to bring that old you back. I'm sorry. I know that's devastating news, but I'm not going to pull the plaster off slowly as I'd be hurting you a hell of a lot more and for a hell of a lot longer.

> 'One always has to know when a stage comes to an end... Closing cycles, shutting doors, ending chapters – whatever name we give it, what matters is to leave in the past the moments of life that have finished.'
>
> PAULO COELHO

Whether you can believe me right now or not, no matter how amazing you think the old you was, the new you, post-treatment, is way better. I know that's hard for you to see or believe, considering how bad you're feeling, but you're only feeling like this because you've lost a sense of who you are – or, at least, you think you have. However, as you begin to understand that in fact you haven't lost a sense of who you are, that you've just transformed into somebody different, you can gradually let go, move on and start to explore and discover the new you. And as you do, the bad feelings you're struggling with now will disappear into the past along with that bloody awful cancer treatment.

You haven't lost yourself. You've just changed and become somebody new.

Becoming a butterfly

While you were busy surviving treatment, a magical transformation was taking place within you: a metamorphosis into your true self.

Now, really think about the magnitude of that for a second.

Most people remain one person their whole lives, but through the negative experience of cancer treatment you have the opportunity to rediscover yourself, to peel back the layers and connect with the very purest part of you that's probably been buried for most of your life. Isn't that amazing?

I am so much more now than I ever used to be before my diagnosis. I am a butterfly: I am light and delicate but also strong and powerful; I am a magnitude of colours that reflects inwards on myself and outwards to the world around me; I no longer just 'live' – I soar. I don't get so wrapped up with the small stuff, because I can fly high above it and get a better perspective. I'm no longer entangled in the drama, in the anxiety, in the fear and depression, because I have learned to let go and just float on by. I love myself more now than I ever have before. I believe in myself; I like the person I have become; I am proud of myself and I accept myself, 100 per cent, exactly the way I am.

My life before cancer was great, but if I compare that life to the one I have now, post-treatment, I wouldn't go back there for all the money in the world. No, really: if you told me you could rewind my life so that I never had to go through cancer treatment, I would say thank you – but no thank you.

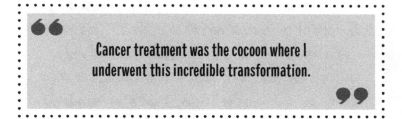

66

Cancer treatment was the cocoon where I underwent this incredible transformation.

99

I know you may feel convinced that the person you were before cancer was so much better than the person you've been left as. You may be feeling, *There's no way I'm a butterfly now.* But wait until you get to the end of this book, and then see how you feel.

I'm not saying your life before cancer wasn't great. And I know it may be very hard for you to believe that the old you was actually the caterpillar and that the person you are today, damaged and bruised from the trauma of treatment, is actually the beautiful butterfly. I know it's hard for you to see that now, but you are just going have to trust me on this.

Cancer treatment didn't take your beauty, your identity or anything else. Yes, going through that trauma changed you but, contrary to what you may believe right now, it didn't change you for the worse – it changed you for the better.

'You can be shattered and then you can put yourself back together piece by piece. But what can happen over time is this: You wake up one day and realize that you have put yourself back together completely differently. That you are whole, finally and strong - but you are now a different shape, a different size. This sort of change - the change that occurs when you sit in your own pain - it's revolutionary. When you let yourself die, there is suddenly one day: new life. You are Different. New. And no matter how hard you try, you simply cannot fit into your old life anymore.'

GLENNON DOYLE

The old you no longer exists. That's a difficult fact to accept but it's unchangeable. It's time to stop looking back and start getting to know the new you, right here, right now. When you start to let go of the past, when you willingly release the old version of yourself, you will be able to emerge from the cocoon, spread your wings and start to fly.

I know right now it seems all too easy for me to say this to you, but remember I was once exactly where you are. I was confused and I was lost; I hated the person I had become through my cancer experience – she was unfamiliar, and that felt strange and incredibly uncomfortable. And to feel that way is perfectly normal.

But as you let go of the old you and get to know the new, your perspective will, slowly but surely, start to change. You'll spend less time missing your old life and more time looking forward to the prospects of your life today. You'll actually start really digging yourself and begin to realize that your life from here on in is going to be amazing.

Change isn't bad. Transformation isn't bad. Growing, evolving, learning and renewing: these are the things that take our lives to a new level, the things that open our eyes to a whole new way of being, to experiencing a peace and happiness we never knew existed.

Right now, you probably believe that if you let go of who you were before the cancer, then you might disappear altogether. But that couldn't be further from the truth. Letting go of the old version of you is the only way to allow yourself to discover who you've become. Letting go is about closing the door on what was before and allowing yourself to open a new door to what is now.

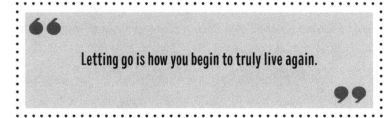

Letting go is how you begin to truly live again.

You're not giving up anything and you're not losing anything. You're a brand-new you. A little bit imperfect and a lot more beautiful – and you don't have to fit back into the person you used to be. It's time to move on, and it only takes one person to change your life: you.

May the old you rest in peace

The only way I could truly move on and find some peace and joy in my life was to say a final farewell to who I had been. And you need to do the same. So, it's time for some good old-fashioned acceptance. This is your moment, your opportunity to truly let go and embrace who you really are today.

Are you ready?

Good, because it's time to say *your* final farewell – a eulogy to who you used to be. Your eulogy will celebrate the life of the person you were before being diagnosed with cancer. And it will be the starting point for your healing process – your way of letting go, of saying goodbye, so you can stop looking back and start looking forward.

Your eulogy will provide you with an opportunity to honour the memory of who you used to be; and, with love, to leave that person in the past, where they belong. The action of writing your final farewell will give you the closure you so desperately need in order to shut the door on the past and finally walk through the door to your bright future.

Now, before you think I'm completely mad to suggest this, I'm not the first person to use this technique in order to bring closure, clarity and transformation. The practice goes back many years and is often recommended by therapists and life coaches as a tool for letting go and moving on. Steve Jobs, for instance, recommended that top business executives should write their own eulogies in order to gain clarity on what kind of person they were and what kind of person they truly wanted to be. Daniel Harkavy, who coaches business executives, says, 'When we take time to write our eulogies, it creates this magnetic pull power that draws us forward. Our priorities... come into sharp focus. This clarity enables us to make the best decisions, get up out of our comfortable patterns... and start moving us towards a better future.'*

I'll tell you now that a eulogy is not an easy thing to write, as those who have ever written a eulogy for a loved one who has passed will know – and it's even more daunting and overwhelming writing one for yourself when you're still alive. But, as I mentioned earlier, transformation isn't an easy and pain-free process, and if you truly want to get yourself to a life of peace and happiness then you'll be willing to do whatever it takes.

I myself found it incredibly hard, but it was also the first truly effective and cathartic step I took towards moving on and being happy. Writing my eulogy enabled me to let go of trying to go back, and to finally make peace with the fact that part of me no longer existed. Once I'd done it, it felt as though a massive rock had been lifted from my shoulders and that I could finally start to move on and feel positive and hopeful about my life and what lay ahead.

* Grothaus, M. (2018), 'How Vividly Imagining Your Own Death Can Help Your Next Career Move', *Fast Company*, https://www.fastcompany.com/90266043/how-vividly-imagining-your-own-death-can-help-your-next-career-move [last accessed 3 August 2020]

I let go of so much when doing this exercise. I let go of desperately clinging to the way my life was before cancer; I let go of self-pity; I let go of the resentment and anger I had towards cancer and, most of all, I let go of this stupid need to let it define me for the rest of my life. My eulogy was the start of my journey to truly loving myself and finding joy and light in my life after surviving the hell of cancer treatment.

I'm going to share with you my eulogy to the old me so you can get an idea of what I'm asking you to do. Yours doesn't have to be anything like mine, and you don't have to show it to anybody. This process is for you; there is no right and wrong, just as long as you connect with your heart, get brave and express whatever you feel inside.

Eulogy to the Old Me

She died suddenly, sitting in an armchair facing the specialist who'd just told her she had breast cancer. One minute she was there; the next she was gone. She suffered no pain in her passing, she just disappeared.

I knew her better than anyone else did. I knew her inside out and upside down, and even though she was far from perfect, she was everything to me and I feel lost and empty without her.

I didn't appreciate her as much as I should have; I took her for granted because I assumed she would always be there. I wish I'd had the chance to tell her more often how awesome she was, to wake her up every morning with a smile and say, "I love you, Saskia. I really love you."

She always felt she wasn't good enough or didn't look the way she wanted to. And yet, now, I realize she was imperfectly perfect just the way she was. I realize she was way too hard on herself and spent way too much time pulling herself apart instead of building herself up.

She spent way too much time sweating the small stuff, dwelling on the superficial things that, in the big picture, really don't mean anything at all - like silly arguments with friends or keeping up with the latest fads - instead of seeing how much was right in her life and everything she should have been grateful for.

I'm going to miss her fantastic cleavage and her super-long, wavy beach-blonde hair. She believed those two things were her identity - the things that made her worthwhile, gave her confidence and self-worth. But really those things didn't do any of that; the confidence and self-worth she believed was hers, due to her tits and hair, was superficial and never real. She never understood the true meaning of self-love, and so she could never see all the loveliness that she was.

I'm going to miss her sense of freedom, her sense of invincibility and her readiness to conquer the world. I'm going to miss her crazy rock 'n' roll spirit that got her dancing up on the bar, downing shots of absinthe while singing into an empty beer bottle to a drunken crowd. I'm sad that I won't see that part of her again, but I smile gratefully because I got to live some of those crazy, crazy nights with her.

She is gone now, and I must say goodbye - goodbye to her, goodbye

to the old me. She is not dead; she
has just moved on and let me go
on without her. Before disappearing,
she left me with a gift of love: a
new, clean white page and a boxful of
technicolour crayons with which to draw
a new life for myself.

She is the old me, and it is time for
me to draw a new picture of myself.

Rest in peace, old me.

Now it's your turn. Please don't shrug this off and continue with
the rest of the book. If you do, then nothing is going to change.
You chose to read this book because you're struggling, and this
exercise is an integral part of your journey in reaching a place
of joy and peace after cancer treatment.

⇒ YOUR EULOGY TO THE OLD YOU ⇐

Writing your own eulogy might seem daunting, but it's often when we
face what we find daunting and scary that we reap the greatest rewards.
It doesn't matter how long your eulogy is – it could be a single paragraph
long; it could be 20 pages. This is your journey, your process. You'll know
when you're done, because something in you will feel different.

It's OK to say goodbye to the old you. You won't disappear – I promise.

1. Find a safe space

Designate a special time and place for this exercise, somewhere you'll have peace and quiet and where you'll be undisturbed for at least an hour. Put your phone on silent and make sure there will be no other distractions. Our nature is to avoid what makes us feel uncomfortable, so your subconscious may start trying to find ways to avoid this exercise – a beep from your phone or some dust on the carpet might be all your mind needs to persuade you to do your eulogy another time. Be aware this might happen and try not to give in to it. When you suddenly think of a call you forgot to make or something you need to add to the shopping list, catch yourself, smile to yourself and let it go. This exercise is way more important than any of those distractions; this is to do with the rest of your life. Having said that, if you do get distracted, don't beat yourself up about it. You're trying to make yourself feel better, not worse, remember? Just get back to it as soon as possible.

It may help to get away from familiar surroundings, from your office or home, where you know there'll be distractions to tempt you away. I took a notepad and pen and sat on a bench in a beautiful London park. Watching the birds and squirrels, being surrounded by the beauty and sounds of nature, helped me to become more reflective, to really look deep within and connect with my feelings. (However, if you think this exercise may bring on tears, and the idea of crying your eyes out and snot trickling from your nose in a public park is somewhat unappealing to you, I completely get that. So perhaps cosy up in your favourite safe place at home and do it there.) Go somewhere that feels right and that resonates with you, whether that's a park bench, your bedroom, a quiet cosy café, a busy bar or on top of a mountain – wherever you feel you'll have a better and clearer perspective and can allow your creativity to flow.

2. Be 100 per cent honest

There's no point doing this exercise if you're going to be all polite and reserved about it. Just say what you feel. If you loved every little thing about who you were before the nightmare of cancer treatment swallowed you up, then say that. If you weren't your biggest fan, then be honest about that too.

Write down the things you'll miss most about the old you, and the things you're actually quite relieved to let go of. Describe your favourite and worst bits about your old self. Write about how you were funnier back then or had awesome hair; or that you were a superficial airhead (like I used to be), or self-centred, or impolite. Just feel it, think it and write it. This is your chance to get some closure, so make sure you express everything.

3. Connect with yourself and feel it all

This may sound easy to do, but in fact most of us struggle to truly connect with the emotions bubbling up inside of us. Perhaps, as a child, you were told it wasn't right to be emotional, that you shouldn't think or write about how you feel; perhaps having feelings at all was frowned upon. But this is an emotionally charged exercise that will make you feel all kinds of things: sadness, regret, relief, peace, anger – the list could go on and on. There are no wrong or right feelings. What's wrong is not allowing yourself to feel it all, so please give yourself permission to feel absolutely everything.

If tears start coming up, then let them come; let them pour down your face. Stop caring about what everyone else thinks or any 'stiff upper lip' nonsense. This is medicine for your soul, and crying is the kindest thing you can do for yourself because it helps you to release the pain and negativity you've bottled up inside and really start to heal.

Maybe you'll meet some resistance within yourself when doing this exercise – maybe after your first few attempts you'll rip out the page, scrunch it up and throw it away in a temper. That's OK, too. My eulogy took me a few attempts, during which I became frustrated and irritated, felt stupid and uncomfortable. Part of me was fighting back – part of me didn't want to say goodbye – and so the words didn't flow naturally. But I didn't give up. I kept trying until I overcame the resistance within me. I may have had ten balls of scrunched-up paper by my feet, but I kept on trying. So, don't give up: no matter what emotions come, allow yourself to feel them and keep on writing.

4. Don't worry about how it sounds

This isn't a writing competition; you don't have to submit this as an assignment. This eulogy is for you and you only. No one else has to see it. You may be a terrible writer, you may suck at grammar – who cares? It's of no importance here and no one is judging you. What you're doing is brave and courageous. What you're doing takes some serious guts. To write a eulogy for the part of you that no longer exists – that's a big, brave deal. So, don't put even more pressure on yourself by thinking it has to be perfectly written. This exercise is about getting rid of all the negativity; getting all the sorrow, grief and frustration out of you once and for all, so you can finally start to move on.

You can do this. And trust me, once you do, your powerful wings will start to open and you'll finally get to know the beautiful butterfly you have become. It's over to you now; please don't read on before you've finished your eulogy.

Time to grieve

So, you wrote your eulogy. How does it feel? I wish we could be sitting face to face over a cup of tea and you could tell me all about it.

I hope you weren't expecting instant happiness and peace, because, sadly, a healing journey like this doesn't quite work like that. We are slowly shifting things around, removing obstacles, clearing out the old and bringing in the new. This takes time and patience, one step at a time. But writing your eulogy to the pre-cancer you is a giant step, so pat yourself on the back and show yourself some love. Be proud of yourself: you just shifted the direction of your life.

Now comes the next step: you need to give yourself permission to grieve. Grief is a natural response to loss, and in order to truly let go and move on, you need to give yourself time to feel that loss. When someone who has been a major part of our lives is suddenly no longer with us, we allow ourselves to mourn. So, feeling profuse sorrow for the loss of someone we used to be is completely logical and completely acceptable.

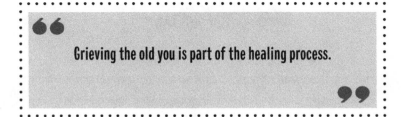

> Grieving the old you is part of the healing process.

I fought hard not to let go of the old version of me and refused to go through the grief and sorrow in what it meant to truly move on. But I eventually discovered that I had to grieve the loss of my old self just as I would grieve the loss of anyone else I had loved and lost. I had to stop putting on this brave face, pretending it didn't hurt. You, too, need to allow yourself to feel the pain of saying goodbye to the person who was most familiar to you, the one you knew better than anyone else. You need to feel the sadness, the loneliness and the loss in that.

There's a ritual that can be of help to you in this process. Perhaps the word 'ritual' conjures up images of witches dancing under the moon or of human sacrifice, but I assure you that is not the kind of ritual I am referring to. In reality, we all have rituals that we use on a daily basis to bring us comfort in some way, like the reassurance of drinking a warm cup of tea made exactly the way we like it. We perform mini rituals all the time. These rituals provide us with a sense of safety, meaning and connectedness. And in times of grief we need some sort of ritual to help us to let go and move on.

In this simple ritual, you physically let go of your old self by burying the eulogy you have written, finally putting your old self to rest so you can move on.

⇨ RITUAL BURIAL ⇦

Find a special place in your garden or somewhere else outdoors where it's OK to dig a small hole. Bury your eulogy in the hole, perhaps laying a flower over the top as you say your final goodbyes. (Alternatively, if you don't have access to green space, burning the eulogy is equally effective, but make sure you do this safely and responsibly.)

Let this ceremony give you a sense of closure. Once your eulogy is buried (or burned), it's time to move on.

―――――――――――――

With your eulogy completed and buried, the person you were is gone. You have accepted this; you have said goodbye and you have grieved your loss. Now you can finally start letting the new you emerge. You can watch as the person you transformed into starts taking shape. The cancer cocoon has gone, and all there is now is the butterfly that you've become.

Hello Me, nice to meet you

The old you has been laid to rest, and here you are with the person you are today – the new, post-treatment version of yourself. So, don't you think it's a good idea to really get to know who that person actually is?

When you start a new relationship – whether it's with a roommate at university, a work colleague or a new romantic partner – you take your time to get to know that other person, right? You ask them questions, you notice what they like to wear, what they eat, what their hobbies are, what they like to talk about, and so on.

Your relationship with the new you is no different. You need to start from scratch, just like with any other new relationship. How cool is that? How many people do you know who ever take the time to really get to know themselves? We all just grow up in our families, schools, societies and cultures and are told, taught and influenced about who to be, how to be, what to think and how to feel. And later on in life, we never question any of that; we pretty much just accept it. We take for granted that these things really are what define us, determine how we feel and how we see the world. But perhaps, if we had the opportunity to take a moment to really think about who we are and what we're into, we'd discover that in actual fact these things aren't us at all; it's all just what we've been told, what we're used to and what we've come to accept.

The idea of meeting yourself all over again might seem strange, but please don't be put off. This getting-to-know-you process is a good thing – no, it's a bloody great thing. Most people get stuck with the same old them their whole lives, but someone who goes through a huge traumatic ordeal like cancer treatment gets to meet a whole new version of themselves and start a whole new, fresh relationship with the newly transformed person they've become.

There are things I used to love doing before my cancer treatment that I feel totally differently about, now that I've become the new and improved me. For instance, I used to love wearing high heels and had a pretty impressive collection of them; I was more than happy to spend a ridiculous amount of money on some sexy stilettos. But after my cancer ordeal, I didn't want to squash my feet into those painful torture contraptions any more. I figured I'd been through enough pain with chemo needles and a mastectomy. So, now I find stylish footwear that doesn't kill my feet; I still dress funkily, but I've given all my high heels to my best friend. I don't miss them at all, and my best friend is very happy indeed. That's not to say I'm suggesting you get rid of your designer shoe collection. I'm just saying that's one of the things I've done as a consequence of going through cancer treatment.

Here's another one: I used to love a long, hot bubble bath at night with a cold glass of wine, as stress relief and a way of relaxing. But my post-cancer medication now gives me the most horrendous hot flushes, so lying in a hot bath for more than ten minutes just feels sweaty, uncomfortable and the complete opposite of relaxing. Also, nowadays I don't drink like I used to – and, for some reason, post chemotherapy I just don't like the taste of white wine any more. So, for the person I am now, sweating in a hot bath then adding a glass of white wine into the mix would see me spontaneously combust all over the bathroom walls. What used to be my idea of pure heaven is now my idea of pure hell, and certainly wouldn't help to relieve stress. This is perfectly fine, but I've I had to work out what helps the post-treatment me to de-stress.

Chemotherapy can really play havoc with your taste buds. During chemo, I craved foods I never ordinarily ate; and after chemo, the foods I used to love made me nauseous. For example, every time my mum drove me to chemotherapy, I would insist on the way home that we stopped at my favourite gelateria so I could get three scoops of their hazelnut ice cream that had lashings of Nutella-like goo in it. Before chemotherapy I didn't even like ice cream. Or Nutella. Weird.

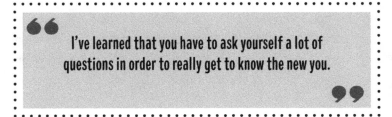

I've learned that you have to ask yourself a lot of questions in order to really get to know the new you.

If I don't like the things I used to, then what do I like now? What does the new you like to eat? What's your go-to comfort food or favourite thing to order on Deliveroo? What kind of lifestyle is more suited to the person you are today – are you a fitness fanatic or is your preferred exercise a long walk through the woods in your wellies? Even the kind of music I listened to changed after my treatment, from loud party and rock music to a more spiritual and folk-style vibe.

And getting to know the new you isn't only about discovering what's changed – it's also about realizing which parts of you aren't worth holding on to any more, such as the old, negative behaviours and defects you've been carrying with you for way too long. I cringe to admit it, but I was pretty selfish and self-centred before the hell of cancer treatment. Nowadays I couldn't be less like that person if I tried. The new version of me has dedicated her life to helping and supporting others. Talk about a 180-degree flip in attitude! Now is the opportunity to let go of the parts of yourself that no longer serve you, or didn't even serve you in the first place. I didn't want to be a selfish git any more, so I made the decision not to be.

You may find you don't have much in common with the old gang of friends you used to hang out with all the time. That doesn't mean I'm suggesting you cut those people out of your life, but you don't have to hang out with them every weekend, either. I don't hang out with the people who dedicate most of their social life to drinking, because I'm not that into drinking any more. I still stay in touch with a lot of my old crew on social media, but the friends I have now have much more in common with the person I've become. I discovered the changes in myself and, as a consequence of those changes, my lifestyle and the people around me have changed too.

> 'Shifts in taste and perception frequently accompany shifts in identity. One of the clearest signals that something healthy is afoot is the impulse to weed out, sort through, and discard old clothes, papers, and belongings.'
>
> JULIA CAMERON

Consider this part of the book your time to 'weed out, sort through, and discard' and to discover the new parts of yourself. I hadn't a clue I'd changed so much until I sat down and did the exercise I'm about to give to you. You've done the hard bit, of letting go and grieving; now it's time to meet the person you've become. So, get ready to get to know you. Here you get to discover your tastes, likes, dislikes, value system and so on, and start to establish who you are and what you're into now, right here, after everything you've been through.

Below is a profile you need to fill in, just like one on a dating website, only the questions here are geared towards you getting to know all the beautiful intricacies of who you are as a consequence of going through treatment.

⇨ GETTING TO KNOW ALL ABOUT YOU ⇦

Below are your 'dating profile' questions. They encompass everything, from what you believe in, to what you like doing for pleasure, your life purpose, how you want to live, what food you want to put in your body and what music into your ears. You can answer all of them or just choose the ones that resonate with you, but know that this only works if you're willing to work it. Real happiness starts with a true understanding – an accepting and embracing – of who you are, right here, right now.

So, grab a journal, a notebook, or a napkin if need be, and start getting to know you. Remember to direct these questions to the person you are today – the person who survived cancer treatment. Don't answer the questions from the perspective of the old you – you let go of that person, remember? This exercise is to help you get to know who you are *now*, so be prepared for your tastes, outlooks and preferences to be different from before you were diagnosed.

Most important of all, be honest with yourself, because the only person you'd be lying to is yourself – and what's the point in that?

Take your time and have fun. Think of it as going out on a first date – with yourself.

Your questions

⇨ What would your perfect day look like?

⇨ What are three things that can put a smile on your face, no matter what?

➡ What do you do to relax and unwind?

➡ Name five things you could never do without.

➡ If all jobs had the same pay and hours, what job would you like to have?

➡ Are you a morning person or a night owl?

➡ Are you an extrovert or introvert – or a bit of both?

➡ What activities energize you?

➡ What activities make you feel depleted?

➡ What new activities do you want to try?

➡ What are five words that best describe your personality?

➡ What personality trait do you value most about yourself?

➡ What personality trait do you dislike the most?

➡ If you could eat only one particular food every day for the rest of your life, what would it be?

➡ What song, band or genre of music cheers you up when you're down?

➡ What kind of movies are you into?

➡ What kind of books do you like reading?

➡ If you unexpectedly had a completely free afternoon, what would you do with that time?

➡ What does the word 'spirituality' mean to you?

➡ Who do you like hanging out with?

➡ Where do you feel safest?

➡ What's your most valuable possession?

➡ If you could trade lives with one person for an entire day, who would it be and why?

➡ What would your perfect holiday look like?

➡ If you could write a quick note to your younger self, what would you tell them?

➡ In what situations do you feel most out of place?

➡ What are you most grateful for?

➡ Do you prefer spontaneity or planning ahead?

Your answers will create a kaleidoscope of colours describing who you have become. They will show you how you have transformed, no matter how small or vast those shifts and changes may be. Now look over your answers and get familiar with this person, because you're going be hanging out with them for a while!

In the next chapter I'm going to introduce you to another part of yourself; a part of yourself that's always been there, though you may not be too familiar with it or how it's been wreaking havoc on your life. Get ready to meet: the ego.

CHAPTER 3

The Ego Is a Troublemaker

There are a lot of people who say you need the ego in order to survive; that the ego is there to protect you, to keep you safe from harm. But I don't believe that's true. I believe the ego is the inner-critic voice within us that instils negative feelings such as self-doubt, anxiety, fear and not feeling good enough... to name just a few. I believe the ego disguises itself as you, so you'll believe everything critical that it says. But the real you, the voice that you *should* be listening to, is hidden deep within, and the only reason you never realized it was there is because the ego has been shouting so loudly you couldn't hear it.

Some people give the ego a capital 'E' when writing about it, but I'm not going to because the ego is already arrogant and full of itself, and I'm not going give it an even bigger head than it already has! It should be just a small 'e' for ego because we need to let it know it's not the be all and end all of our existence, that we are no longer willing to listen to all of its nonsense and we are most certainly no longer letting it rule our lives.

So… let me get the bad news over and done with right now: the ego lives within you and it isn't going anywhere. It will always be there. The good news is there's another voice within you – your soul – and you get to choose which voice you pay attention to. Your soul is who you really are, and therefore that's the only voice you should be listening to.

But here's the problem: the ego lives in your head and the ego speaks the loudest. Your soul voice resides in your heart and doesn't feel the need to shout and scream; it speaks calmly and quietly. So, in order to hear your soul, you must first learn how to quieten down the ramblings of the ego.

> **66**
>
> **It's time to stop assuming that the ego is your friend and that the ego has your back, because it isn't and it doesn't.**
>
> **99**

By looking at your relationship with the ego up until now, and having the willingness to shift your ideas and thoughts about it, you can start to transform your life in all the right ways. It's about recognizing that the ego's volume has been up way too high and realizing that all you need to do is turn it down so you can start connecting to what's really going on. By following the guidance and tools I offer in this chapter, you can learn to ignore the ego's rantings and ravings, and to tune in to what your true self is trying to tell you.

I'd spent my whole life thinking the ego was me and believing everything it told me, and as a consequence my life wasn't all that great. But once I realized that the ego isn't me, that the ego voice is not my own, I learned to tune in to what my soul was saying and I never looked back; I've never been happier. Now, whenever I feel a negative emotion creeping in or a negative thought popping into my head (like the fear of the cancer coming back, or that I am less than the person I used to be), I have the tools to turn the ego volume down and the soul voice up, transforming those negative thoughts and emotions into positive and uplifting ones.

Whether or not you want to believe it, your true voice – your soul voice – speaks within your heart and is a voice of pure love. It is a voice that unconditionally loves, accepts, inspires, forgives, encourages, nurtures and supports.

But you can't hear that voice, can you? You did once, albeit a very long time ago. The very moment you were born, you came into this world as pure love. As a baby you didn't know anything about negativity, you didn't know what it means to feel insecure, jealous, anxious or less-than. As a small child, you completely, 100 per cent believed in yourself; you believed you could do anything and be anything, like an astronaut or a fairy, or both at the same time. In your imagination you could fly, talk to the animals and become invisible whenever you wanted to. Everything was possible.

But then the world got hold of you. You started to be conditioned by your parents, your upbringing, your schools, your society. You experienced competition, comparison, criticism, judgement and the need to conform and fit in. The day came when you stepped out into the 'real' world and it started to fill your head with all its rules and regulations. And all of a sudden, that beautiful, innocent imagination you once had was replaced by logic, and the ease of being happy and carefree was replaced by practicality and responsibility. And as this change occurred, your inner critic, the ego, was born and started to grow. Its voice started to get louder and louder until, inevitably, it drowned out your true voice – your soul voice – altogether. This didn't just happen to you – it happened to each and every one of us.

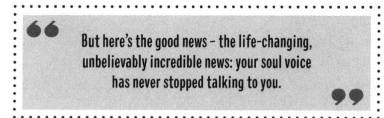

But here's the good news – the life-changing, unbelievably incredible news: your soul voice has never stopped talking to you.

It has stayed with you throughout your life – it's always been there, you've just been unable to hear it. It has kept on trying to speak to you, only the ego has kept drowning it out. But it has never given up. Your soul voice has waited patiently for you to wise up to what's really going on so you can finally turn the volume down on the ego and hear that true, sweet voice of love and positivity again, just as you did when you were a young child. I did it, and though I know it may be hard to believe, I now hardly ever hear the negative thoughts and I hardly ever say a bad word about myself. If I do hear them, I now know how to turn down the volume of that negativity to barely a whisper. I learned how to control the volume so I can decide which voice I hear inside of me. Sure, some days the ego screams and shouts so loudly that it's all I can hear and I start believing its rantings and ravings. But then I remember that there are two voices and I have a choice which to listen to. Just by having that awareness, just by knowing what the ego is up to, I can choose to put it on mute and get on with my day.

I am not saying I've obliterated the ego from existence – I wish I was that powerful. I'm not saying that I don't sometimes get sucked in by the ego's cynical comments or by the lies it whispers to me. But whereas I used to struggle with that negativity almost every day, now I hardly do at all. The journey of life is about progress, not perfection; it's not about abolishing our defects and struggles, it's about being aware of them and doing the best we can to deal with them. You'll never make the ego disappear completely, but you can keep its mouth shut the majority of the time and you'll be blown away by the difference this will make to your life.

So, what does this have to do with cancer and your journey after treatment? Everything and nothing. By getting a handle on the ego, not only can you truly let go of all the negative talk that keeps you stuck in your cancer treatment experience, but you can let go of the old thoughts and feelings in your life that have always held you back and prevented you from being truly happy.

So, first things first: how do you tell the difference between the ego voice and the soul voice?

Easy. If you feel fear, anxiety, dread, jealousy, resentment, regret or anything else negative and crappy, then that's the ego.

If you feel acceptance, peace, hope, light and positivity, then that is your real voice – the voice of your soul.

Can it really be that simple? Yes, it really can.

The ego is judgemental, arrogant and negative, and tends to

focus on anything fear-related. The ego is a master at blaming, criticizing and complaining, and in making and justifying excuses.

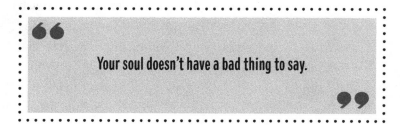

> **Your soul doesn't have a bad thing to say.**

Your soul is an optimist that always sees the bright side of life. No matter what struggles and obstacles come your way, your soul has your back; it searches for the solutions and will do whatever it can to make you feel better, think better and live better. The soul uplifts, empowers, commends, approves, applauds and continually compliments. Your soul connects to everything and everyone; your soul is pure energy capable of tapping into all the magic and wonder, the positivity and vibrance, the hope and possibility, that life has to offer. Your soul is all about enabling you to connect, to experience, to create and to benefit from this big beautiful world of ours.

So, tell me, which voice would you rather listen to?

Know your enemy

To conquer the ego, you need to know exactly who it is you're dealing with. Who is this inner critic and lover of all things doom-and-gloom who's messing with your life? To do this, it's imperative that you first separate yourself from the devious little bugger, by giving the ego a distinct identity of its own. This makes it easier to separate its voice from yours. You will then stop believing the ego is you and that the thoughts and feelings it whispers to you are your own.

This is the tool that truly set me free. It was only when I learned to differentiate between my true self and the ego that I started to fully appreciate myself and stopped beating myself up or putting myself down. It was also only then that I realized it had never been me beating myself up in the first place; it was never my own words, thoughts, feelings and beliefs that were consuming me with fear; I never hated myself – but the ego did a fantastic job of convincing me that I did.

After cancer treatment, I was plagued by the words of the ego:

➡ *I am nothing compared to who I was before I got cancer.*

➡ *I'll never feel as beautiful as I did before cancer.*

➡ *I am broken and damaged now.*

➡ *Everyone who hasn't gone through cancer is so much luckier than me.*

➡ *I'm ugly now.*

➡ *Who's going to love me, knowing I went through cancer?*

The ego always speaks in the first person, so it sounds like it's you that's doing the talking. What a crock of poo! Let me tell you right now that the ego is the most cunning and devious creature you will ever have to deal with. There is no man, woman, child, animal, rock, mineral, tree or sea monster you will ever meet that is as dark, pessimistic or challenging. And that's good news, my friend, because it means if you can conquer the ego, you can conquer any challenge that comes your way.

Think of some of the horrible things the inner-critic ego says to you: the cruel put-downs that it says about you or the people around you; the fearful thoughts and ideas it puts into your head; the regrets or longings for the past or anxieties about the future. Now use your imagination to give the ego a face and a name that's totally different from yours, imagining what kind of creature would say such dark and sinister things.

Ever since I gave the ego a face and a name, I hear the negative talk but immediately know that it's not me saying it. I simply imagine the ego sitting on my shoulder whispering its malicious sweet nothings into my ear, and instantly I know it's not me being negative, dark, judgemental, fearful or critical; it's the ego. Freedom!

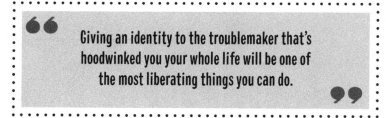

> **Giving an identity to the troublemaker that's hoodwinked you your whole life will be one of the most liberating things you can do.**

My ego looks like Gollum, that weird, hairless, long-fingered annoying creature from the movie *Lord of the Rings* who keeps saying 'My precious...' in a creepy, slimy voice. My ego looks like him and sounds like him; that's who popped in my head when I tapped into those negative thoughts and feelings. So, now, if I hear any words of nastiness or negativity in my head, I simply picture Gollum, that slimeball deviant, sitting on my shoulder, twiddling my hair with his fingers, wearing a big grin on his face, whispering into my ear and corrupting my soul. I know it's him bugging me and that I don't have to believe any of the negative crap he's going on about.

I used to be plagued with fear about my cancer coming back. If I got a headache I'd immediately think, *What if it's spread to my brain?* I'd have a scan and think, *They're going to find something sinister.* But now I know that it wasn't my own fear that was putting those thoughts in my head, but a fear created by that troublesome ego. So every time those thoughts creep into my head now, I just imagine it's Gollum trying to convince me of those things and I tell him to shut the f**k up! I no longer believe any of the vicious put-downs or criticisms; nor do I heed any warnings of doom and gloom. And you don't have to either.

Whenever those thoughts or feelings of negativity are starting, I tell the ego to bugger off and leave me alone. It may sound insane, but it works. I know it sounds crazy and it's probably very much outside your comfort zone. But how's your comfort zone been working out for you so far? Maybe, just maybe, it's time to try something new and see if it works. So, next time you get overwhelmed by fear, or start comparing yourself to somebody else, or tell yourself you're ugly or broken, try to imagine the ego sitting on your shoulder whispering those things into your ear. By doing this simple exercise you will, slowly but surely, train yourself to realize that those thoughts, fears and feelings are not your own.

You've probably spent your whole life believing what the ego tells you, so it's going take some time and practice in order to shift those deep-rooted beliefs. But you can shift them. Giving the ego an identity separate from your own, and imagining it whispering all the negative stuff in your ear, is the first step in that process.

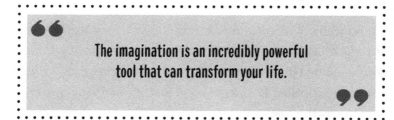

> The imagination is an incredibly powerful tool that can transform your life.

We don't give the imagination enough credit for what it's capable of doing. Your imagination is tapped into parts of you that you didn't even know existed: parts of yourself that go beyond body and mind; parts of yourself that can tap into the flow of life, to the Universe, and create profound and beautiful changes. I'm not exaggerating: your imagination can make magic and bring miracles into your life.

Do you remember when you were little and used to play in imaginary worlds? I do. I remember being a princess and feeling like the most beautiful girl in all the land. I remember being a pirate who was all-powerful and owned the Seven Seas, and a pop singer who was number one on *Top of the Pops* every single week. In my imagination, I could achieve anything and be anyone, and just because I'm now middle-aged, it doesn't mean the power of my imagination has changed.

We can use our imagination to transform the way we think and feel, no matter how old we are. So, all I am asking is that you try to reconnect to that part of yourself, to the days when you allowed yourself to make believe, the days when you created magic from your own imagination. Use your imagination and give an identity to the voice that has been lying to you all of your life.

Maybe your ego is a big weird blob of black slime; maybe your ego is an evil hedgehog whose spikes are made out of titanium nails; maybe your ego has horns and is half man, half animal; maybe it's green, or red – or both! It doesn't matter what face or name you give to the ego; what matters is that you finally differentiate yourself from it so you can finally be free of its darkness, fear and negativity.

It's time to stop believing everything you think.

The ego as saboteur

Do you ever feel like there is something holding you back? Something that's preventing you from living your best life and being the best version of yourself you can possibly be? Do you have negative thoughts, beliefs or feelings but, deep down, know they're not actually true? Have you ever done something that you knew would be detrimental to your wellbeing, but you did it anyway?

Well, guess what? You are very much not alone. We all do it.

We are led to believe that these kinds of feelings and behaviours are forms of self-sabotage; that we are inflicting wrongdoing, wrong-thinking, pain and struggle on ourselves. But I don't agree. Let's look at some of the dictionary definitions of the word 'sabotage':

'Things that are done to stop someone from achieving something or to prevent a plan or process from being successful.'

MACMILLAN DICTIONARY

'To deliberately spoil someone's plans because you do not want them to succeed.'

LONGMAN DICTIONARY

Why do we believe we do this sabotaging to ourselves? Why are we so quick to believe this kind of negativity is self-inflicted? It makes no sense. Think about it: you wouldn't destroy your own plans because you don't want yourself to succeed. You wouldn't maliciously prevent yourself from being happy and living your greatest life. I mean, what would be the point of that? Why on earth would we blame ourselves? There has to be another explanation – and there is.

> 66
> **It's not you who's sabotaging yourself;
> it's the ego that's doing it.**
> 99

You're not inflicting the negativity, the struggle and the fear upon yourself; it's the ego up to its old tricks again. Why are we so quick to add the word 'self 'in front of the word 'sabotage'? Why are we so quick to blame ourselves for all the times we make a bad decision or allow fear to stop us dead in our tracks?

Enough of blaming ourselves, people!

Sabotage is the ego's way of keeping you small and fearful, and under its control. It's the ego that's been causing all the trouble but it has very conveniently managed to convince us that we bring these things upon ourselves. I'm so fed up with all of us believing that it's we who have screwed up our lives. It's time we stopped blaming ourselves and start pointing our fingers at the real culprit... The ego.

'The more you can have control over your ego rather than let it run amuck, the more successful you'll be in all areas of your life.'

ROY T. BENNETT

This whole time, you thought it was you beating yourself up, putting yourself down, criticizing and judging others, thinking the worst, dwelling on the past and fearing the future. But I'm telling you loud and clear that it ain't you! And the way to stop the ego sabotaging your life is simply to wise up to what's really going on, so you can take back your beliefs, thoughts and feelings and no longer let the fear, anxiety, insecurity and negativity control your life.

The ego's armoury

The ego is a terrorist with a full armoury of weapons that aim to keep you small, fearful and separate, and unable to ever hear the true voice that resides deep within you. The ego's knives, guns, grenades and bombs are sadness, fear, anxiety and resentment.

But imagine a life that's no longer controlled by negativity, criticism, doubt and fear. Doesn't that sound like heaven? Well, take it from someone who knows: freeing yourself from the ego can be done, and it most definitely does feel like heaven. But before I give you the tools to turn down the ego's volume to an insignificant murmur, you need to be aware of the weapons it uses to keep you stuck.

Machine Gun of FEAR

 This is the ego's number-one weapon of choice. It's the weapon that causes the most damage; that defeats, beats and wins every single time.

FEAR: False Evidence Appearing Real

I want you to memorize my words for what 'FEAR' stands for: False Evidence Appearing Real. Say this over and over again until you believe it, because the knowledge that fear is simply false evidence, which the ego uses to hoodwink and manipulate you, is your bulletproof vest.

The ego uses fear to shut us down, to stop us becoming the

best and happiest version of ourselves. The ego fires its fear machine gun continually in our direction so that we never truly get up and stand in our own light. Instead we are scared, lying on the floor too afraid to move.

As soon as you realize that fear is a weapon that the ego uses against you, the sooner that fear ceases to have power over you. From here on in, you can make the decision to stop being so damn afraid.

Perfection Bomb

Perfectionism has nothing to do with perfecting yourself, with making yourself the very best you can be, but the ego disguises it as that in order to keep you stuck in a perpetual quest for something completely unattainable so you never feel good enough. We naively believe perfectionism is an honourable trait and yet it's just another weapon the ego uses against us.

Perfectionism is not a good thing. In fact, there is no such thing as 'perfect' – it's a concept created by the ego so that you waste your time on an eternal quest for something that isn't real. Researchers have actually proven the downside to perfectionism: all it does is cause a long list of health problems such as anxiety, lack of self-worth, depression, eating disorders, insomnia and chronic headaches.* This alone should make

---

* Ruggeri, A. (2018), 'The Dangerous Downsides of Perfectionism', *BBC Future*, https://www.bbc.com/future/article/20180219-toxic-perfectionism -is-on-the-rise [accessed 3 August 2020]

you wise up to the fact that perfectionism is just a bomb the ego is using to destroy you, to distract you from being truly present and noticing that actually you have a lot going for you right here, right now.

Messing up, going the wrong way and making bad choices are all a necessary part of transforming into our greatest selves. Sometimes it's the messing-up that rewards us with the biggest life lessons, the ones that transform our lives forever. If you avoid making mistakes, if you're always trying to do and be perfect, you hold yourself back and keep yourself stuck. And who is it that loves holding you back and keeping you stuck? Bingo! The ego. You see? You're already starting to wise up to what's really going on.

By realizing that the perfectionist thoughts and feelings you have are not your own then you have all the bomb-disposal knowledge you need to prevent the perfection bomb from exploding and causing damage in your life.

Anger and Resentment Rocket-Launcher

 Nothing will steal your happiness and wellbeing faster than anger and resentment, and that's why the ego adores these rocket-launchers so much.

Initially you'll detect just a little disturbance, irritation or discomfort, and if we didn't listen to the ego these things would stay small and manageable. But the ego starts to whisper, to provoke, and to turn that cute little molehill into a mountain that's 10,000 times bigger than Mount Vesuvius and is just waiting to erupt hot molten lava over everything and destroy your world.

Yes, getting cancer sucks. I know it and so do you. But resenting the fact you got cancer and feeling angry about it: where's that going to get you? Nowhere but knee-deep in the sinking mud of negativity. It's the ego's way to make sure you never actually move on.

So, next time you feel anger or resentment brewing, stand your ground and refuse to be blown away. Picture the ego standing right in from of you and tell it to p**s off while displaying your middle finger and a big happy smile on your face. Refusing to get sucked into that toxic, negative energy is the best way to stop the ego dead in its tracks and turn it into the meaningless, insignificant speck of nothing that it really is.

Anxiety Uzi

Oh, yes, indeedy: the ego loves a bit of anxiety; it loves seeing you in such a tiz that you almost forget to breathe. Anxiety is the ego's way of separating you from everything and everyone, because when you feel anxious you get lost in your own craziness. It's as though you become oblivious to reality, which is just how the ego wants you.

The ego wants you so overwhelmed and anxious that you simply give up, hide and don't bother trying any more. But the truth is that you can handle anything and everything that life throws at you. It may not feel like that – you may feel as though the Universe has buried you under a gigantic mound of pungent negative poo – but you can make it through. How do

I know? Because I managed to do it when I was drowning in a vast ocean of crap, and, my darling, if *I* can, so can you.

So, when you next get sucked up into the mayhem and turmoil of anxiety, remember it is just the ego's Anxiety Uzi firing bullets at you at 1 billion miles per hour and from all directions. And just being aware of this will make those bullets disappear into nothing.

Criticism and Judgement Sword

What's the best way to stay miserable?

1.   Criticizing and judging yourself

2.   Criticizing and judging other people

3.   Criticizing and judging yourself and other people at the same time

By criticizing and judging ourselves, the ego makes sure we never ever feel good enough. By criticizing and judging others, the ego makes sure we come from a place of disconnection and fear. And by doing both at the same time, we are just royally screwing ourselves over.

If you want to irritate the hell out of the ego, simply do the following. When you look in the mirror and are about to insult yourself or put yourself down, give yourself a compliment instead. So, in that moment when you look at the state of your hair in the chaotic 'growing out' phase after chemo, don't dwell on the negative of that; instead, just tell yourself it's funky and wild. As soon as you do, the ego's sword of criticism and judgement turns flimsy, floppy and useless. Do the same with other people, too: when you look at someone and start judging or criticizing them in your head, make the choice to mentally compliment them instead. For example, the other day I was sitting on the train and a woman opposite me had the hairiest legs I've ever seen. My ego was sniggering and whispering, 'Yuck, look how disgusting her legs are. It makes my skin crawl, it's so gross.' But then I chose to shut the ego up by focusing on my heart and connecting to my soul voice. So instead I chose to think, *I have to give that chick credit. She clearly doesn't care what anyone thinks and does what's right for her. I wish I was that brave.*

At those times when you're being critical and judgemental, looking in the mirror or at other people and picking apart what you see, remember it's not you that's doing the picking. Because why on earth would you belittle and destroy who you are, or get pleasure from belittling and destroying somebody else? It makes no sense. No, it's not you doing the destroying, it's the ego that's telling you your bum's too fat, her legs are too hairy or you look crap with a pixie hairstyle.

Past and Future Stink Bomb

Now this one seems harmless enough. What's wrong with reminiscing about old times or looking ahead at things to come? There's nothing wrong with either of those things.

But the ego takes the past and future and turns them into one hell of a stink. It's OK to reminisce about days gone by, but not if you think all your best and most beautiful moments are behind you. And it's great to get excited about what's around the corner, but it ain't so great to be sitting in the present, preoccupied with the doom and gloom of when you might die.

So, if you catch yourself fearing the future or missing the past, take a sniff and realize the ego has just chucked a smelly Past and Future Stink Bomb right at you. Focus on something in the here and now that can get you back to the present and the ego's stink will immediately start to fade away.

See how easy it is to ignore the ego and the sinister weapons it uses to alienate you, separate you, belittle you and keep you down? In every moment you have the choice to wise up to what's really going on, to who's doing the talking in your head, to choose not to listen and to tune in to what your soul thinks, instead.

Now you'll know immediately that when you're feeling something that's detrimental to your wellbeing, it's the ego that's doing the talking. This acknowledgement and awareness will be the forcefield that stops the ego from hurting you any more. You can't permanently rid yourself of the ego, but you can take back the control in your life and protect yourself from believing everything the ego says.

Surviving the ego

So how do you fight back against the ego's grenades, bombs and bullets? Simple: you don't.

Fighting for peace is a contradiction in terms. The ego is the violent one and you can't beat violence with violence. By loving yourself, by acknowledging how worthy you truly are, by building yourself and others up and not putting yourself or others down, and by refusing to believe the lies: that's how you stop the ego's weapons from hurting you.

The fact the you can never be rid of the ego is actually a really good thing. Wanna know why? Because as long as the ego tries to pull you into the darkness, to think the worst, to feel bad, to dwell on the negative, you will always consciously have to work on doing the opposite. By being aware of the ego and its tricks, you will teach yourself to focus on the light, on the positive, on goodness and beauty. The ego is actually helping you to become the greatest version of yourself.

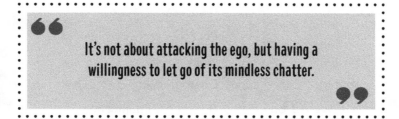

It's not about attacking the ego, but having a willingness to let go of its mindless chatter.

By knowing you have an ego disrupting, discouraging, poisoning and pissing over everything, you can choose to believe differently; you can change your thoughts, you can let go of negativity and you can be ridiculously happy.

The thoughts and feelings you really have don't live in your mind, where the ego resides, but in your heart. That's where your soul voice is, and the first step to surviving the ego is to stop focusing on what your head tells you and to start paying more attention to the ideas, thoughts and feelings that come from your heart and that are the messages from your soul.

Ego voice or soul voice?

The following list will help you distinguish the ego's traits from those of your true soul's nature. Knowing which voice is which will immediately give you the power to choose where to focus your attention. By choosing to listen to one voice, you are letting the other voice go.

Ego	*Soul*
Separation	Connection
Doubt	Faith
Confinement	Freedom
Victim	Owning your power
Self-pity	Positivity and cheerfulness
Repress	Release
Closed off	Open-minded
Passive aggression	Honest communication
'Should have...'	'Could have...'
Suppression	Creativity
Worry	Hope and anticipation
Resentment	Letting go and moving on
Resist	Accept
Excuse-making	Ownership
Guilt	Forgiveness
Anxiety	Courage
Struggle	Flow
Avoidance	Willingness to try

'This is the end'	'This is just the beginning'
'A waste of time'	'A lesson learned'
Fear	Love

It's completely up to you where you want to dwell – on the left-hand column with the ego or the right-hand column with your soul. At any point, in any moment, you always have the choice.

Controlling the volume

There are several handy tools and tips to help you turn down the ego volume and finally tune in to the calm, quiet and peaceful voice of your soul.

The body-focus

We mistakenly assume if we're getting messages and thoughts from our mind, then it's got to be us talking, but your true soul voice doesn't live in your headspace. In fact, the voice of your soul – your higher self, your spirit, and the voice you can trust – comes from anywhere *but* your head. So, to hear your soul voice, instead of thinking and feeling from the neck up, try thinking and feeling from the neck down:

➡ Neck up: Ego voice

➡ Neck down: Soul voice

Just by shifting your focus to a different part of your body, you can decide which voice you'd prefer to listen to.

People connect to their soul voice in all kinds of ways. Take the following phrases:

'Gut feeling'

'Belly knowing'

'Feel it in my bones'

'Gives me goosebumps'

'Follow my heart'

'Having a funny feeling'

'To know in your heart of hearts'

'Tingling in the spine'

'A feeling in the pit of your stomach'

My own soul voice is in my heartspace, so whenever I get overwhelmed by the negative chatter in my head, I focus on my heart and listen to what the voice there has to say instead. Its words are always positive, loving and uplifting, completely contradicting everything the ego in my head is trying to convince me is true. But you might feel and hear your soul voice somewhere else. There's no wrong or right here – all that's important is that you take the focus away from the head and zone in to the area where you find your true intuition and guidance.

If you're hearing the ego chattering in your head, be still and transfer all of your attention to where your true voice speaks to you. Now ask your soul what you *really* think and feel. I guarantee if you redirect your attention to where your soul voice resides, you will discover it has something completely different to say.

Creative visualization

The imagination is a superpower that each and every one of us was bestowed with, and you can use it to overcome and achieve anything. So, use the power of your imagination to keep the ego quiet.

Imagine the ego standing in front of you – the ego you gave a face and name to a few pages back (*pages 46–47*). Imagine it trying to convince you of negative things. Now, using your superpower of imagination, visualize taking some gaffer tape and sealing the ego's mouth shut. Now watch the ego go red in the face, with puffy cheeks, trying with all its might to attack you with its spiteful words but not being able to say a thing!

Just by using the creative force of your imagination, you have shut the ego up.

Action improvisation

(Warning: this is best done in private because you will look like a complete weirdo.)

Sometimes the ego is so loud and so damn convincing that I start believing everything it's saying. These are the sort of things the ego shouts at me:

➡ 'You're not good enough.'

➡ 'You're not half the woman you used to be before cancer.'

➡ 'What makes you think anyone out there is interested in what you've got to say?'

➡ 'You're an imposter and will never amount to anything.'

But eventually I catch on to what's happening. Then I picture the ego perched on my shoulder – that Gollum-like creature, all hairless and sinister, whispering evil sweet nothings in my ear. I know it sounds completely insane, but I literally grab that imaginary asshole off my shoulder, chuck him on the floor and stomp on him. I squash the ego to a pulp and shut it up.

No, I don't do this exercise in front of other people; I may be somewhat quirky but I'm not a complete nutjob. So, if you're in a public place when the ego starts beating you to a pulp, just pop into the nearest public toilets, lock yourself in a cubicle, grab that ego off your shoulder and flush it down the loo. Boom! Job done.

Be willing to do something a little bit weird and a lot out of your comfort zone, because this tool could be the one that turns down the volume on your inner critic and prevents you from getting swallowed up by any more fear and anxiety. Trust me, you might feel like a total knob while you're doing it, but the immediate relief and reprieve from the ego's incessant crap is worth it.

Write it away

When the ego's voice is particularly loud and dark, write down its negative criticism, write down what fear is coming up for you and the anger that the ego is trying to convince you is real. Now fold this piece of paper up into a square, put it inside your shoe and put your shoe on. For the rest of the day, make sure you stomp up and down on those negative thoughts and feelings as much as possible. Remind yourself that all the negativity is stuck inside your shoe and cannot get to you. And keep on stomping – take the stairs instead of the lift just so you can stomp that negativity to nothing with every step you take.

At the end of the day, take the piece of paper out of your shoe, rip it into tiny little pieces and flush it down the toilet where it belongs, with all the other crap; or, if you have a fireplace, a fire pit or even a barbecue, once you've stomped on that paper filled with words of negativity, take it out of your shoe and immediately burn it (provided it's possible to do this safely). Just remember to do this very consciously; to really focus on the power of the act. As you put the words of negativity and fear into the flames, watch them burn to embers and be conscious that as that paper disappears, so do all those toxic thoughts and feelings.

The more you practise these slightly kooky techniques, the more you'll learn how to turn down the volume of the ego, of the fear and negativity, and start hearing all the love, possibility and positivity that your true self is trying to tell you. Remember, you have the power to switch your focus from your mind and the ego to your heart and your soul.

CHAPTER 4

When the Going Gets Tough, the Tough Get Spiritual

When I found the willingness to open myself up to getting to know my spiritual side, I found all the tools and wisdom I needed to heal myself and to love me back to life.

Ralph Waldo Emerson said, 'What lies behind us and what lies before us are tiny matters compared to what lies within us.' And he was 100 per cent right. The cancer treatment is in the past, and the future isn't quite here yet, but our power and beauty are within us right now, and that's what we should be focusing on. I know you might not believe you have power or be able see your beauty yet, but by the end of this book you will.

Don't be afraid of the word 'spiritual'. Don't immediately assume that it has to be inextricably linked with a church, mosque or temple, or that anything to do with spirituality is interconnected with the word 'God'. Of course, it can be, and for some that's exactly what it is, but it doesn't have to have anything to do with God or religion. If you went out today and asked each person who passed you on the street to describe their idea of spirituality, they would each have a different answer. You get to choose what spirituality is and means to you.

For me, being spiritual is about believing that underneath who we think we are – underneath our character and personality, the colour of our skin, our gender, religion, fashion sense, thought patterns, behaviours, beliefs, health issues, financial situations, family background, culture, and so on – we are all, at our very essence, one and the same. We bleed the same red blood and we cry the same wet, salty tears. That's what spirituality means to me – but it could be completely different for you.

Spirituality is how I got to see the beauty and power inside me, to believe in myself and fall in love with who I am now, after what I went through. But I never used to be spiritual. In fact, I didn't have a spiritual bone in my body. I didn't have a clue about 'connecting' with myself; I didn't even know what that meant. I was as disconnected as they come. I was way too busy focusing my attention on the things outside myself: shopping for yet another pair of sexy heels I didn't need, watching another episode of my favourite TV series, keeping up with the latest fads and face creams. I didn't think about looking within, because, quite frankly, I didn't think I'd like what I'd find in there. So, I focused my attention on anything above the surface and never dared to go deep. I had no relationship with myself, so I had no relationship to anything remotely spiritual, either.

But after being diagnosed with cancer, the things that used to preoccupy me stopped meaning so much and I started looking for something more. Buying an expensive pair of shoes or hanging out in the trendiest new bar just didn't give me the buzz it once did. Cancer made so much of my life meaningless, and forced me to face those parts of myself I'd been avoiding for years.

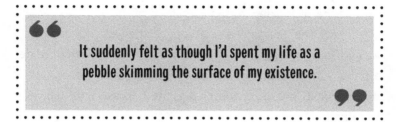

It suddenly felt as though I'd spent my life as a pebble skimming the surface of my existence.

But now I felt the need to tap into something bigger, and I was willing to venture into the heart of myself to find it. Stripped bare, without my looks to depend on, without my busy life to hide behind, I realized I had never really taken the time to get to know who I am. So, I started to explore the whole notion of spirituality as a means to get to know myself better, to explore all the different aspects of who I am. And what I realized was that spirituality was the door I had to open so I could step out of my comfort zone, away from the superficial way I'd been living my whole life, and discover all the hidden treasures that lie in the darkest depths of who I really am.

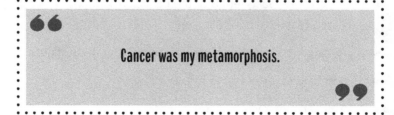

Cancer was my metamorphosis.

My own spirituality started just with the willingness to try something new. I knew I was unhappy and I was willing to do anything not to be unhappy any more, so I started exploring spiritual stuff even if I didn't understand what it was. I read books, I tried meditation (even though I totally sucked at it), I tried yoga, I listened to podcasts. This was my first real experience of looking within – instead of looking everywhere else – for the happiness, confidence, peace and answers I longed for. And the more I explored who I am inside, under all the other crap like cancer, insecurity, my background, the colour of my skin, and so on, the happier and happier I became.

The spiritual path took me to parts of myself I didn't even know were there, and allowed me to see how much awesomeness has been hiding in me this whole time. Following a spiritual path has allowed me to:

➡ find my life purpose

➡ experience a peace and joy I didn't previously know existed

➡ fall head over heels in love with myself instead of fixating on falling head over heels with somebody else

➡ learn to accept everything I am – even the bad bits

➡ let go of the past, let go of the cancer treatment, let go of regret, resentment and anger

➡ no longer be consumed by fear, anxiety, guilt or shame

➡ stop being fearful of the future

➡ discover the power of forgiveness

➡ let go of needing to control everything in my life

➡ no longer look outside myself for happiness and confidence, because I found it all within me

It sounds like a lot, but that's what spirituality gave me – no word of a lie. I literally felt magic starting to happen, and to this day that magic keeps on happening.

That doesn't mean I don't have bad days or even bad weeks. It doesn't mean my life is perfect and that I never get upset or stressed or fearful or angry. But it does mean I have all the tools I need to handle those things. It means that I don't feel alone any more. I no longer feel like I am carrying the weight of the world on my shoulders all by myself. And now I have a spiritual connection, I know I'll never feel isolated and alone again.

For me, spirituality, and living a spiritual path, is simply a way to heal myself from the inside out. It is the development of my heart, mind, body and soul by learning to connect with myself and with a power greater than myself.

Tapping in to your spiritual side will:

➡ teach you how to stay in the present moment so you are no longer plagued by longing or regret of the past, or by fear and anxiety of the future

➡ help you to overcome fear and to realize that you yourself have the power to make yourself happy

➡ offer you clarity when you feel overwhelmed and confused

➡ inspire you to believe that anything and everything is possible; and, by believing this, making it so

➡ show you how to believe in something bigger that can hold, guide and support you

➡ make you feel excited about life and all the mystery and beauty that is yet to unfold

➡ give you a sense of peace that is always there, deep within you, no matter how chaotic things become

➡ show you how simple and easy life can be if you just choose differently

➡ introduce you to the most beautiful parts of yourself – parts of yourself you didn't even know were there

➡ allow you to tap into your own intuition and guidance so you can find the answers yourself, instead of asking everyone else for their opinion

Sounds good, right? So, if you want to explore the spiritual path, follow me...

Higher Power who?

Your Higher Power has always been, and will always be, with you.

Many people associate a 'Higher Power' with a dude in a white robe, with a long beard, who hangs out on clouds. For many people God is their Higher Power. But not for everyone. Your Higher Power can be anything you want it to be, as long as you consider it to be a kind of super-duper being, spirit or power that is much, much greater than you, me and all of us put together. The trick to living the happiest life you could possibly live is to be open and willing to believe in something.

That something could be the Universe, God, nature, Mother Earth, the ocean, the sky, Buddha, Yoda, Universal Energy, Dumbledore or Jesus. It could be something undefinable you don't even have a name for. It doesn't matter what you call it, just as long as you call on something.

The moment I was willing to believe in something else, something bigger than me – that's when my life started to change. Whether or not I believed yet in this Higher Power wasn't the point; at the beginning it was simply about having the willingness to consider the concept. Once I was willing to believe in a power that I might not understand but could nonetheless trust was there, that's when my spiritual journey really began. As soon as I made the choice to trust and believe, to connect with something greater than myself, all of the broken pieces of my life started fitting back together. And not only that, the pieces fitted back together in a way that made me more whole than I ever was before; that made an even more awesome and beautiful me.

Alan Cohen, in his book *Spirit Means Business*, describes it like this: 'Higher power is the invisible hand that orchestrates your success. When you partner with that power, events that would otherwise be painstaking become doable and even easy.' And that, in a nutshell, is what happened to me as soon as I gave this whole Higher Power thing a go.

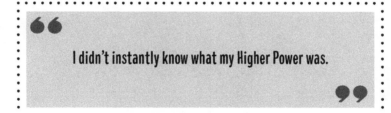

I didn't instantly know what my Higher Power was.

It took time, exploration and an open mind for me to work out what a power greater than myself meant to me. I started with the idea that everything in the whole Universe is made up of energy. That's a fact I can't dispute because it's been scientifically proven. So, in essence, everything and everyone is made up of the same universal energy: you, me, the chair I'm sitting on, the trees and birds I can see outside my window, the guy from Amazon that just dropped off a package at my door and the package he delivered. Everything is connected, everything is part of this universal life force, everything is made up of the same stuff. So, I made that my Higher Power: the energy or force that is in absolutely everyone and everything. Believing that made sense to me, and it was, most definitely, a power greater than myself.

Over the years, my concept of a Higher Power has evolved and transformed. The idea of 'God' has always been a tricky thing for me. I grew up in a non-religious household where the most influential people in my life didn't believe in God, so I never really had a clue about him/her/it/them. But as I've progressed down the spiritual path, I've created my own definition of what God is and what God means to me. Now, my Higher Power is that life energy that runs through all of us, and through the Universe and God. What I'm trying to say is that you can make your Higher Power anything and everything, just as long as it resonates with you and your beliefs.

⇨ WHAT IS YOUR HIGHER POWER? ⇦

What does a power greater than yourself mean to you? If you're not sure, then consider doing the following to help you find out.

Ask others their beliefs

Speak to your friends, speak to other cancer survivors, and find out what it is they believe in. You might not agree with their outlook or beliefs, but something they tell you might just resonate and connect.

Look to your own religion

If you believe in a particular faith path, then you've already got your Higher Power sorted – God, Jesus, Allah, Buddha, Krishna... The deity or deities of your religion are a power greater than yourself that you are already connected to.

Meditate on it

Find some quiet time to be alone with yourself and think about the concept of a Higher Power. Sit on a park bench surrounded by nature and ask yourself what it is you believe in. Then give yourself the time and space you need to hear the answer.

Do some research

Sit with your faithful and trustworthy old friend Google, and ask 'What is a Higher Power?' See what pops up. There's endless inspiration online for what a power greater than yourself could mean to you.

How to connect

How can you tap into the superpowers of the Universe? What methods can you use to connect to your Higher Power? First of all, you need to close your eyes... and jump.

Much like a trapeze artist who must willingly leap into the air with arms outstretched to reach the bar, you need the same willingness to take the leap of faith that something will be there to catch you. Because not only is your Higher Power the net that will catch you if you fall, it is also the bar you are reaching for and the force behind your leap of faith.

But how to jump? You can do so with thoughts, with feelings and with actions; with the simple willingness to try new things and to do things differently. Each time you allow yourself to think a new thought, to feel differently or do unfamiliar but spiritually aligned actions, you'll bring yourself closer to that powerful universal source. It's not a simple click of your fingers and – abracadabra – you are perfectly in tune with a Higher Power. If it was like that you wouldn't get to enjoy the beautiful journey, the magical carpet ride of finding your spiritual path.

There are several tools and methods you can use to start building your spiritual connectivity. The following small, but ever so powerful, practices will help you to reach a state of being where you can create a true connection between yourself and your Higher Power on a moment-to-moment basis.

Please try all of them. You can only know something doesn't suit you if you try it on first. So, try everything on for size and see what fits. Just like when you go clothes shopping; you may take ten items into the changing room and try them all on, but you may only end up buying two or three things.

Wake up and say thank you

As soon as you open your eyes in the morning, before you get out of bed to pee, say thank you. Thank your Higher Power for a good night's sleep, or a warm, cosy bed, or for the people in your life. I'm sure you can find something to be grateful for. Doing this means you connect with your Higher Power first thing and raises the chances that you will stay connected throughout your day.

Prayer

Prayer is a silent conversation in your head that you have with a power that you believe in. That's it. It's just reaching out and chatting to your Higher Power. Kinda like this: 'Hey, Higher Power, I'm really struggling today. I feel overwhelmed with thoughts of my cancer coming back. Any chance I can hand this stinking thinking over to you? I'd really appreciate it.'

Prayer is the way most people begin their connection to their Higher Power, and most of the time they don't even know who or what it is they are praying to; they're just ready and willing to start the conversation. It's like meeting a stranger and feeling absolutely no connection at first, but gradually, after a few chats, you start getting closer and the bond starts to grow. There's no right way to do it: the important thing is to start the dialogue – say hello and see what happens. You'll be amazed by how the relationship slowly but surely starts to form. One word of advice, though: don't only have a natter with your Higher Power when you want something or need help. You need to be consistent in order to create a strong bond. It's also very important to give your Higher Power a big high five when it positively impacts your life. If you acknowledge and praise the good stuff your Higher Power does, then it knows what you want more of and it will start to bring more of it about.

Be aware of signs

Your Higher Power sends you messages in all kinds of weird and wonderful ways, but if you haven't yet been connected then you won't have noticed. Stay alert, because these signs happen all the time. A book falls open at a page you're supposed to read, someone on a TV show says something that resonates with your soul, a song playing on the radio may have a lyric that answers a dilemma you've been battling with or reassures you all is OK when you're riddled with anxiety. I've got into my car feeling overwhelmed and down in the dumps, then put on the radio in the middle of the Beatles belting out 'All You Need is Love'. And I giggle to myself because I know the Universe is telling me to cheer the f**k up!

We're all so quick to say something is coincidence or luck, but there ain't no luck or coincidence when it comes to your Higher Power. Your Higher Power orchestrates all the magic, all the positivity, all the answers. You just have to take off your blinkers and pick up on all the divine messages you're receiving.

Just sit quietly

Connecting with your Higher Power can be as simple as finding five minutes to sit quietly and making the conscious decision to reach out. Find a safe, cosy and peaceful spot, even sitting on the bathroom floor with the door locked if that's the best sanctuary you can find. It's essential that it's quiet, because it'll be very difficult to tap into your Higher Power if you've got the TV blaring or the kids demanding your attention. Quiet is where we create the strongest bond, the most powerful connection, to source. If necessary, wear some noise-cancelling headphones; you could also play some calming instrumental music to help you tune in.

Then just close your eyes and make the intention to connect to your Higher Power, trying to feel that universal force all around you. Trust me, just having this intention is enough. Even if you don't feel that you're connecting to anything, you will be. You don't need to feel shivers down your spine or be illuminated by a divine white light. Your Higher Power doesn't need all those gimmicks; its subtlety is where its power lies. So, don't overanalyse if you can't feel it. Just be.

Be childlike

I am giving you permission to act like a kid. How does this help you connect to your Higher Power? Well, think about it: when you're an innocent little kid, you're open and receptive to anything. You believe in fairies and Santa Claus; you believe anything and everything is possible. Returning to that childlike state makes you completely open and receptive to the Universe and all the gifts it wants to bestow upon you.

When you're in a childlike state, you forget about your fears, you forget about the past and future; you're completely present and focused on what you are doing right now. When a child has some paints, a brush and a blank piece of paper, they're not worrying about what to have for dinner or if the ice cream van is going to drive past tomorrow. They're simply immersed in that blank paper and its endless possibilities. A child has the beautiful ability of being 100 per cent present, and it's that part of yourself I'm suggesting you tap into, because it's in the present that you're at your most receptive to connecting to your Higher Power.

So, go and sit in your garden or in a park and tune in to your childlike self; whisper sweet nothings to the flowers or hug a tree. Get back to the little one you used to be before you got consumed by being an adult. The wonder and innocence you once experienced as a child are still there. To tap into them again, all you have to do is play like a child. It's from that pure, childlike place that you can connect to your Higher Power with complete ease and naturalness.

Find the Universe already in your life

Serendipity is one of my favourite words. It means good luck in finding valuable things unintentionally. If you find good things or magical things happen to you without looking for them or deliberately making them happen, then serendipity has brought them to you. And another word for serendipity, as far as I'm concerned, is Higher Power. I don't think good things are just coincidence – I think it's your Higher Power smiling down on you.

We've all experienced moments of serendipity; like when 10 cars are all looking for a parking space but as soon as you drive into the car park a space opens up right in front of you. Or you lose your wallet, then some lovely stranger taps you on the shoulder with your wallet in their hand and ask if it belongs to you.

What if you started believing that these magical occurrences are your Higher Power proving to you that it exists?

Physical movement

Strolling through the forest, running through the city, dancing under the stars or sweating it out at the gym can all be ways to connect with a universal force. Physical activity influences the spiritual aspect of your life. It makes your heart rate increase and your body release endorphins, which trigger a positive feeling throughout your body. In a nutshell, physical movement makes you feel alive and feeling alive connects you to your Higher Power. Exercise can also allow you that much-needed alone time, without distractions; a space to connect with your Higher Power. Some people call it 'Me time' but I prefer to call it 'Me and my Higher Power time'. As you are walking or jogging, focus on nothing but your movement, the power and energy of each and every step. Be aware that this energy is connected to something greater and all-powerful that enables you to put one foot in front of the other and keep on going.

Connect to community

Sometimes, in order to connect to a Higher Power, we need only connect to other people. Joining a local support group, sports club or charity organization can be an effective way of opening the door to your Higher Power. Your Higher Power doesn't just work through you; it also works through others, so, you can develop your connection with your Higher Power by connecting with your fellow man. New relationships, new communities and new connections with others open up new connections and vibrations with your Higher Power and the whole Universe.

If you go back hundreds of thousands of years, our relationship to each other, and our connections, were the complete opposite of what they are now. As a species, we thrived through community and tribe. We had a deep sense of belonging, support and acceptance through being part of a group. Your spiritual power grows in connection with everyone and everything, so the more willing you are to become part of a new group or community, the more connection you are creating with yourself and your Higher Power.

Mindful eating

This is one of the easiest and simplest ways to connect to your Higher Power. Instead of just wolfing down your lunch while reading this book, put the book down and pay attention to what it is you're eating and to the blessing of being able to savour its taste and benefit from its deliciousness. Don't eat in a mind-numbing state, because you'll be wasting perfect moments in which to connect with the food and with your Higher Power, which has served it to you.

Next time you eat, pretend it's the first time you've ever eaten that particular food. If it's an apple, hold it in your hand and take in its shape and its texture for a moment. Marvel that something so wonderful even exists. Then bite into it as though you're biting into an apple for the very first time and you should be blown away by the incredibleness of its sweetness and crunch. By putting all of your focus onto the newness of that fruit, you immediately bring yourself into the present moment and still your mind.

Get creative

Anything you do creatively is a sure way to connect to your Higher Power. So, start painting, sculpting, blogging or photographing; do anything and everything that gets your creative juices flowing. Your Higher Power loves communicating with you through your creativity, so express yourself, create from your heart, and allow yourself to be completely open to your Higher Power and its guidance.

These ideas are just to give you a taster of some of the things you can do to start building a bond with your Higher Power. My hope is that they inspire you and make you think of other ways you can start to build a spiritual connection. Remember that by paying more attention to the things you do, you allow yourself to return to the present moment and truly connect with what is. All the suggestions I have made are simply ways to retrain your mind; to allow a connection with yourself, and something bigger than yourself, to grow.

CHAPTER 5

Feel It to Heal It

This book isn't a magic pill and I'm not a magic wizard that can wave a magic wand and make you feel instant magical joy. I promise that if I could do that for you, I would. But the truth is this: the only way to move past the pain and the struggle is to feel it. Otherwise it will stay inside you and you'll continue to hurt. Sometimes you have to go through things and not around them.

Remember, you're going through a very powerful process of releasing the old you and introducing yourself to the person you have become as a consequence of treatment. That's going to bring up a lot of feelings, both positive and negative. But don't just welcome in the positive feelings and avoid the negative ones. You need to feel all of it.

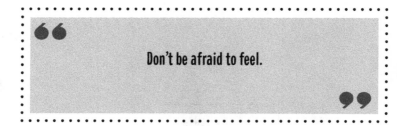

Don't be afraid to feel.

If we do allow those painful emotions to surface and we truly feel them, then – and only then – can we finally be rid of that pain and start to move on, to a bright and beautiful new chapter. But if you don't allow yourself to feel whatever it is that's going on for you, then it stays and it festers, it decomposes, it goes stale and mouldy, and starts polluting your system and poisoning your soul.

For some reason, society has convinced us to believe that feeling negative emotions is a bad thing and to be avoided at all costs. Yes, we are absolutely allowed to jump up and down for joy, jiggle and giggle with excitement, dance with love, beam with confidence and pee our knickers from laughing. But God forbid we cry in public, punch a pillow with rage, shake uncontrollably from sobbing, or curl up in a ball from anxiety. Negative feelings are still feelings, just like positive feelings are feelings. Each and every feeling is normal, acceptable and supposed to be felt.

I'm not giving you permission to throw a chair through a window or scream a profanity at another person when you get angry. I'm just telling you to let yourself feel all your emotions, the good ones and bad ones. We need to give ourselves permission to feel whatever it is we need to feel, and to do so in a productive, safe and healthy way. By facing the emotions we don't want to deal with, we are taking back control of our lives from the ego and liberating ourselves from darkness. When you give yourself permission to feel any and all emotions, you are declaring that there is absolutely nothing wrong, bad or broken about you for feeling them.

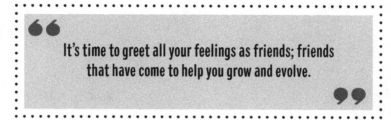

> **It's time to greet all your feelings as friends; friends that have come to help you grow and evolve.**

The negative feelings are not out to destroy you and your life, and they are nothing to feel guilty about. So, it's time to stop running in the opposite direction whenever you feel them and, rather, lean in to them and trust that life is sending you these feelings for a reason.

We must welcome each and every emotion that knocks at our door, because sometimes it's the most uncomfortable and painful emotions that offer the greatest lessons and most profound transformations.

⇨ ALL FEELINGS ARE EQUAL ⇦

Below is a random list of feelings. Go through them and realize that there is not one feeling on that list that is better or worse than another. They are all equally valid, and it's perfectly OK for you to feel any one of them. What's not OK is to deny you are experiencing a particular feeling and to push it down, consequently stunting your ability to be truly happy and at peace with your life and with who you are.

⇨ Love

⇨ Annoyance

⇨ Happiness

⇨ Helplessness

⇨ Elation

⇨ Doubt

⇨ Empathy

⇨ Sadness

⇨ Excitement

⇨ Disappointment

⇨ Amusement

⇨ Dread

⇨ Hope

All the above emotions are acceptable and justified, and you have full permission to experience all of them. But you could say that the negative emotions are the most important to feel, because by doing so we shine a light on the darkness within us, and that is how we heal and transform our lives to find true peace.

I used to avoid the negative emotions at all costs, believing that avoidance would prevent me from feeling the pain. But the only way to overcome and survive negative emotions is to feel them. You need to feel in order to heal. It really is as simple as that. Tears pouring out of your eyes like torrential rain, snot dripping out of your nose and that ugly cry-face are what will ultimately set you free. I now know that if I don't accept the negative feelings then they stay inside and the pain remains constant. The only way past the crappy feelings is to go through them. Now is the time to face the feelings and emotions you have pushed down and hidden away since being diagnosed, so they can come up to the surface and finally be released.

'Your emotions make you human... Even the unpleasant ones have a purpose. If you ignore them, they just get louder and angrier.'

SABAA TAHIR,
A TORCH AGAINST THE NIGHT

It's so important that you stop avoiding negative feelings just because they're uncomfortable; they're just feelings, and you won't die from them. Just let them rise up and out of you. Feel them for a little while and eventually that feeling will dissipate and move on.

Taking the plunge

Imagine you are standing on an island; it's very small and completely barren. Nothing grows there and there are no other people, and no food. You are there all alone, and you're scared and lonely. In the distance you can see another island that is green and lush. You can hear people laughing there and music playing. But in order to get to that place, you have only one choice – to swim, because there is no boat in sight and no one else on your island to help you.

The water that separates you from all those happy people looks dark and scary. So, what should you do? Should you stay alone and miserable on your small, barren island, or should you pluck up the courage to swim through that dark water to make it to the other side?

Make the right choice, people.

Like the ocean you must swim across, there is no way around your negative feelings; you have to swim through them to get to the happy place.

If you're afraid to bring up those feelings after repressing them for so long, then be self-loving and responsible, and reach out to someone. That's what therapists, counsellors, doctors and healers are for. If you don't want to cry on your own, if you're scared to scream all your anger out, then go to a professional and tell them that. Tell them you want to get all those dark feelings out of you, once and for all, but you don't know how. They will be able to teach you healthy, effective and safe ways to feel.

How we numb the pain

There are so many tactics the ego uses to make sure we bottle up all that negativity and keep ourselves in darkness. You may not have even realized you've been using some of them to avoid what's really going on. I was the poster child for using anything and everything to avoid the pain I was feeling inside, both before my cancer diagnosis and after. There was pain bashing around inside me, just desperate to get out, but I didn't want to face it, so instead I found ways to numb it. But all that did was make me feel horrible for a hell of a lot longer than I needed to.

Here are a few numbing tactics you may find that you use, possibly unknowingly, so as not to feel negative emotions – the emotions that most need feeling for healing.

Online shopping

Don't get me wrong – I love the luxury of shopping from the comfort of my home. I mean, what's not to like about buying cool stuff from your sofa or while you're on the loo? But there's a difference between making conscious purchases and just buying stuff to distract yourself from uncomfortable feelings that are trying to come up. In particular, that 'Buy Now' button is the worst thing ever invented. It's instant gratification, instant numbing and instant detachment to what's really going on. It gives you no time to pause and reflect. So, next time your finger is hovering over that button, take a moment, tune in to your heart and ask your Higher Power what's really going on for you? Try to pinpoint what emotion it is that you may be running away from. Perhaps leave the items in your basket for 24 hours before deciding whether to go ahead with your purchase.

You'll know whether you're shopping for numbing reasons or not. Do you feel guilty immediately after purchases? Are you truly present when you make them, or in a daze? Are you buying for the sake of it or because this purchase is necessary and comes from your heartspace?

Food

This was always my numbing tactic of choice. Way before my cancer diagnosis, I used food as a means to avoid the dark stuff trying to rear its ugly head. I had an eating disorder for over 15 years of my life: I was bulimic and anorexic. I would either purge whatever I put in my stomach or not put anything in my stomach at all. Let me explain to you one of the reasons why.

My bulimia was a way of getting out all the negativity; of ridding myself of all my inner demons without actually feeling them. I know that sounds weird, but it's almost as though I convinced myself that if I vomited out the food I'd just eaten, then the feelings that were going on for me would come out too. So, I wasn't just physically being sick; I was emotionally vomiting all the negativity out of my body. Only it didn't work. For years the ego convinced me this was the best way to feel better, but it only made me feel worse and dragged me deeper into a dark hole.

The anorexia, meanwhile, distracted me from the negative feelings by giving me physical hunger to feel instead. I couldn't feel frustration, fear or sadness, because all I could focus on was the physical pain of starving myself. One of the ways I managed to overcome my eating disorder was to try something new and very scary: to actually feel whatever emotions were inside me, good or bad.

My own relationship with food was an extreme, but most of us have used food as a means to numb ourselves from negative feelings at some point in our lives. Instead of feeling the fear of upcoming test results, we reach for the ice cream in the freezer; instead of feeling anger after an argument with a loved one, we start scrolling through Deliveroo menus. It's a very common coping mechanism, but it doesn't work. Most of us just feel fat and guilty afterwards, giving ourselves yet more negative emotions to deal with.

So just try to be conscious of why you are eating. Is it because you're loving your body and listening to it telling you it's hungry? Or are you eating for another reason – to numb something you don't want to feel? If you're about to tuck into your fifth doughnut, try to take a moment to see if you really are that hungry, or if you're just avoiding an uncomfortable emotion. Are you eating to fill your stomach, or are you eating to numb a feeling?

And if you skip a meal because you're 'too busy' or 'there's nothing in the fridge', take a moment and try to be truly honest with yourself. Are you really too busy to take ten minutes out to have a snack? Is there really nothing hiding at the back of a cupboard? Or are you trying to distract yourself from a negative feeling that's just begging to be felt?

Television

No, don't worry, I'm not telling you to stop watching your favourite TV series. But I am telling you that if you spend all day watching back-to-back episodes in your pyjamas, without seeing the light of day, it might be because there are some feelings you're trying to avoid.

Watching TV can be a great way to switch off for a little while, especially if your thoughts are doing a Grand Prix in your brain at 200mph. Observing the life of something or somebody else on television can be a great way to take a break from your head and your world. But TV can also be an excuse to escape from connecting with yourself and what's really going on for you. So, next time you've just watched an episode of your favourite show and are about to go straight into the next one, take a moment to connect with your motivation. Are you watching a second episode because you're spoiling yourself and being self-loving? Or are you trying to zombie out and avoid the feelings in your heart?

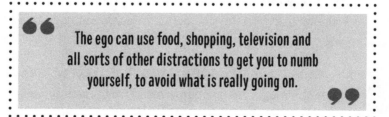

> The ego can use food, shopping, television and all sorts of other distractions to get you to numb yourself, to avoid what is really going on.

All these things can be innocent pastimes or healthy hobbies that benefit and nourish you. But they can also be used to distract you from processing what you're feeling in your soul and your heart. So stay mindful of your intentions. Tune in to your Higher Power and have the self-awareness necessary to know you're doing these things from a healthy place and for the right reasons.

Get off the pity pot

Giving yourself permission to feel negative or uncomfortable emotions does not mean you're giving yourself permission to wallow in self-pity. Self-pity – feeling way too sorry for yourself – can be very self-destructive and pull you even deeper into a dark hole. I may allow myself to feel the negative feelings, but that doesn't mean I run a bubble bath of 'poor me' and bathe in it. Think of self-pity like a swimming pool: you're allowed to go for a swim, but you're not allowed to stay in there indefinitely; until you become a wrinkled-up, miserable prune. It's healthy to do a few laps but don't stay in that pity pool until you drown.

There's a big difference between allowing yourself to feel sadness for the loss of your life before cancer and making that sadness define who you are for the rest of your life. Have a look at these two versions of how you can react to your sadness:

Version A: 'Today I am feeling sad and missing my old life before cancer. It's OK to feel those feelings and I allow myself to feel the sadness so that it may pass.'

Version B: 'Life is so unfair. I miss who I was before cancer and I know I'm never going to be happy again. Nobody understands me, nobody understands the pain and anguish I'm feeling. I might as well just stay in bed and give up on ever being happy again.'

See the difference between version A and version B? Version A is the healthy way of responding to your feelings and Version B is belly-flopping into that pool of self-pity and sinking to the bottom.

I'll be honest with you: after my cancer treatment I did a triple somersault into that pity pool, I let myself sink to the bottom and I lived down there, drowning out all hope of a happy life. I was feeling so much 'poor me, poor me, poor me' that I completely forgot to swim back up to the surface. I was drowning myself in self-pity and wasting a whole lot of precious time.

You want to know how I managed to get myself back up to the surface? I decided to stop wallowing and I chose to swim. The author Elizabeth Gilbert put it perfectly when she said, 'I've never seen any life transformation that didn't begin with the person in question finally getting tired of their own bulls**t.' To be honest, I got bored of myself; I got bored of feeling sorry for myself and lamenting how hard my life was. Wallowing in my self-pity was clearly getting me nowhere except more stuck in the sinking mud of feeling sorry for myself, and I had to get out of it if I was ever going to turn my life around.

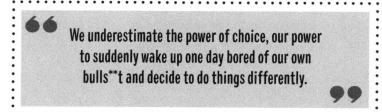

> **We underestimate the power of choice, our power to suddenly wake up one day bored of our own bulls**t and decide to do things differently.**

So, that's exactly what I did: I got so sick and tired of being sick and tired that I decided I wasn't going to splash about in that pool of self-pity any more.

You, too, have that power of choice. If you're feeling sorry for yourself, you can decide right now, in this very moment, that you're not going to feel sorry for yourself any more. Right now, as you're reading this sentence, you can choose differently. You can decide that you're utterly bored and don't want to drown in self-pity any more. You can decide to float up to the surface, get out of that pool of self-pity, dry yourself off and start living your greatest life.

I know this sounds way too good to be true, but changing the way we think and feel doesn't have to be as complicated as we think. Sometimes it can be really simple. Sometimes it can be just a matter of choice. The big question is: are you ready to make that choice? Are you ready to let go of self-pity and move on with your life?

If the answer is yes, then this is it: this is where you leave it, this is where you take back your power, tell self-pity to bugger off and point-blank refuse to take it with you into the next chapter. The following exercises will help you do that.

⇨ A LAST DIP IN THE PITY POOL ⇦

I'm now giving you permission to dive into the pity pool one more time; do a belly flop, a somersault, splash around, do laps, and anything else you want. Just enjoy it, because this is your last swim and after that you're not wallowing in 'poor me, poor me' any more.

I want you to gather up all the juicy feelings of self-pity you can find inside yourself. Stuff like:

➡ 'Life is so unfair.'

➡ 'Why did I have to get cancer?'

➡ 'You don't know how bad it was for me.'

➡ 'Nobody understands what I went through.'

➡ 'Cancer treatment was way worse for me than it is for most people.'

➡ 'I'm so damaged now.'

Have you got all those feelings and all that stinking thinking bubbling up inside you? Good. Now, I want you to take all of those feelings and get rid of them once and for all, using one of the varied ways below – just find one that resonates with you and do it (if you find more than one, even better). What's key here is making the deliberate and conscious decision to release yourself from self-pity. The power is in the action: it's one thing to think to yourself, *I'm not going to wallow in self-pity any more*, but it's another thing to do something hands-on that really manifests the intention. Sometimes, less thinking and more doing is what we need to break down the blocks that keep us stuck. All the self-help books in the world won't help you if you don't occasionally pull your finger out and take some action. Here are your options:

Express your self-pity in words

It could be a poem, a list, a journal entry – whatever works better for you: just write all the self-pity thoughts and feelings out of you and onto paper. As you write, imagine the ink is permanently locking all that self-pity into the paper fibres and there's no way of getting it out. If you want to make doubly sure that the pity stays away, crunch the paper up once you've finished writing and burn it (please do this safely and responsibly). Then there's no way you're going to retrieve that self-pity, because it will have literally disappeared in a puff of smoke.

Paint a pity picture

Draw the feelings and thoughts of pity out of you and seal them in colours and doodles on a blank page. Express all of those 'poor me' feelings and thoughts creatively with paint, crayons or even collage-style, with magazine cuttings. As you're doing it, stay present and be super-conscious of sealing all that pity into the drawing, painting or collage and that once it's in there, it can't come out. Like a fairy tale, imagine you're casting a spell and locking all your self-pity into that picture for ever and ever. The End.

Dance the pity out

Play some music really loudly and dance around your home like a mad person, allowing all those thoughts and feelings of self-pity to dance out of your body and into the beat of the music. Find an uplifting, empowering track (something like 'This Is Me' from the movie *The Greatest Showman*), turn it up as loud as you can bear and as you start moving to the beat of the music, just imagine all the self-pity that's been hiding and lurking inside of you since your cancer diagnosis dancing out of you, and that once it's out, there's just no way it can dance its way back in.

Throw the pity back where it came from

Find a stone and, using a permanent marker, write the words 'self-pity' on it in big bold letters. Then sit in a quiet space with the stone in your hands and imagine sending all of that negative 'poor me, poor me' energy from within you into that rock of self-pity – visualize a dark cloud of pity seeping out of you and sealing itself into that rock. Then go to the nearest body of water you can find – the nearest pond, lake or ocean – and throw that stone into the water with as much force, motivation and deliberate intent as you can muster. That dead-weight self-pity will sink to the bottom, and you can rest safe in the knowledge that it can never find its way back to you.

Scream it out

Climb to the top of a mountain, stand in the middle of a forest or simply squash your face into a pillow – just find an isolated place where you will not be disturbed, and people won't think you're completely mad, and physically scream out all that annoying self-pity with all of your might. Because once you scream it out, you can't scream it back in.

Seal it into a photo

Find a photo that says self-pity to you. Perhaps it's a photo of yourself bald after chemotherapy, or an image that represents feelings of self-pity, like a tree without any leaves or a stormy ocean. Hold that photo against your body and imagine putting into this image all the negative energy from feeling sorry for yourself. Then either lock it away somewhere or rip the photo into pieces and dispose of them for good.

The actions above are simply suggestions to get the self-pity and 'poor me' out of you and into something else. You're welcome to come up with your own ideas – any creative outlet that enables you to release the pity inside yourself and transfer it to something else from which it can never come back. But remember, after you've done this, you can't get it back, because your self-pity from the trauma of cancer treatment is locked in words, stone, song, a photo, a scream or a picture for all eternity, until for ever and never and always and whatever.

Once you've chosen one of these actions, please go and do it immediately.

Yes, right now, please.

Done it? Good. You're not going to milk your cancer-treatment experience for all that it's worth any more, and you don't need to. Because it's bye-bye self-pity, hello bright and beautiful future.

'It's all right to sit on your pity pot every now and again. Just be sure to flush when you are finished.'

DEBBIE MACOMBER, MRS MIRACLE

Your dis-comfort zone

Why on earth do they call it a comfort zone, when it's anything but comfortable? After cancer treatment, all I wanted to do was roll up in a ball, feel safe and not be scared any more. But rolling up in a ball is not safe and it doesn't create a life of joy and peace. I discovered that refusing to step out of my comfort zone actually kept me stuck, sad and missing out on the wonder and beauty of life that I could be experiencing.

In order to move on from the trauma of treatment, you must dare to step out of your comfort zone. That first small but brave step is how you initiate profound and positive change in your life. When I look back over the years, I realize it was the times I boldly stepped out of my so-called comfort zone that I was at my happiest. It was those moments that most positively influenced my life.

After cancer treatment, as soon as I decided to face the fears that were keeping me stuck in a cage that was disguised as safe and comfortable, they immediately started to dissipate and I began to experience a happiness and safety the likes of which I had never known before.

So, you can choose to stay locked up in the way things currently are, in the seemingly comfortable and familiar – or you can venture out of your comfort zone. You can slowly but surely step over that threshold and feel the exhilaration and excitement of experiencing the unfamiliar, of learning and feeling new and wonderful things.

Your happiness, peace, confidence and wellbeing after treatment lies on the other side of fear; it's all waiting for you just outside of your comfort zone. All you need to do is pluck up the courage and take that first leap of faith. Step over the boundary, the illusionary barbed wire the ego has surrounded you with, and your fear will immediately evaporate.

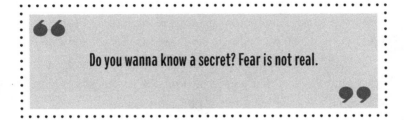

Do you wanna know a secret? Fear is not real.

Yes, the feeling of fear is so overwhelming that it's hard to believe it's simply an illusion. But that's all it is – as we saw in Chapter 3, fear is False Evidence Appearing Real. And the life that you're wanting is on the other side of that illusionary fear.

I know how powerful the emotion of fear can be. After my treatment, I let fear swallow me in one gulp. I gave in, I gave up, I gave out. I allowed the fear to be stronger than me and I caved, and as a consequence everything in my life just got darker and darker, and I got more and more stuck in that zone that is anything but comfortable.

But now, when I feel fear, I know I'm going in the right direction and I don't let the fear cause me to veer off course or stop dead in my tracks. Now that I know fear isn't real, all I have to do is walk straight towards it and its illusionary veil disappears. I know how scary and daunting the thought of leaving your comfort zone is, but taking that risk, taking that first step out, is unavoidable if you want to start living your greatest life.

Being diagnosed with cancer forced you into the unknown; you had no choice in the matter – one minute there you were, standing on solid ground, safely living on the island of your life, and the next you were thrown into the void. Everything familiar and safe seemed to disappear the moment the doctor told you that you had cancer. And now you've got through the treatment, it's understandable that you want to cling on to that solid ground. Now that you've swum back to the island of your life, you never ever want to venture off it again.

But here's the thing: there are so many beautiful places beyond the life you knew, beyond the world you resided upon, before the cancer threw you into the void. There's a big, beautiful world out there, just a step or two outside your comfort zone, so don't let fear prevent you from exploring, discovering, venturing, conquering and truly living. Don't let your comfort zone keep you stuck and don't let fear ruin your life.

Now, then and when

It's something we all have the tendency to do; dwell in the past or project ourselves into the future. We spend way too much time looking back and ahead, instead of seeing what's here right now, in this very moment.

But here's the thing: dwelling on the past or fixating on the future only causes us anxiety, regret, frustration and fear, to name just a few negative emotions. Being in the here and now, however, brings peace, acceptance, contentment, gratitude and a whole suitcase of other delicious and positive stuff.

> 'Yesterday is history. Tomorrow is a mystery. Today is a gift. That's why it is called the present.'
>
> **ALICE MORSE EARLE**

I love that quote – it's simple and so incredibly true. It took me a while to acquire the power of being in the present, but once I nailed it, I never looked back. Previously, I spent way too much time reminiscing about the old me, pre-diagnosis – how much prettier she was, healthier she was, happier she was. But being so preoccupied with the past meant I didn't give myself a chance to see all the good in me, or in my life, right now; to see that, in fact, I was wrong – that the person I am today is even better than anyone I was before, and I've never felt more comfortable in the skin that I'm in. But how I was I supposed to realize that if I was so zoned in on the past? Meanwhile, fretting about the cancer coming back in the future did the exact same thing: it stole away the beauty of my now and all the reasons I had to be grateful in this very moment.

Sure, we can choose to dwell on our past or worry about the future and allow them to define how we feel and who we are. Or we can choose to let go of our past and future and get to know who we are in this very moment, without them. Learning to let go of the past and future to become more focused and aware of the present is truly the greatest gift you can give yourself.

Your life is now. Your life isn't the person you were before the cancer, and your life isn't the next oncologist appointment, either. This moment – this minute, this second – it's all there is and all that matters. Don't waste the present on going back or marching forward. Just for now, just for right now, why not be here exactly where you are? This exact moment is the gift you've been given, so why not unwrap it, take your time, get excited and savour every millisecond.

I'm not saying you have to forget about the past altogether, or that you're not allowed to make plans for the future. Just don't get too preoccupied with what was and what will be, and spend more time with what is.

What are the benefits of allowing the past trauma of treatment to hide the true beauty of who you are today in old memories and regrets? What are the benefits of getting so lost in thoughts of what lies ahead that you're oblivious to all the magic in your life right now?

I always used to think I'd be happy only if and when something happened – when I lost the weight from the steroids, if my hair grew back like it was before, when I met the perfect man, if I became a huge success. We all seem so fixated on this idea – that happiness will happen one day in our future – when in fact we can be happy simply by living in the present. See what I'm saying? Going back or projecting forward just takes us out of ourselves and disconnects us from where we are now.

The cancer treatment is in the past and whatever happens in the future is beyond your control, so why dwell on it? Doing either just makes you lose sight of your present life, and as a consequence life passes you by without you having the chance to really enjoy any of it. Replaying the past over and over again doesn't change it, and wishing things were different doesn't make it so.

⇨ SEIZE THE PRESENT ⇦

Stop worrying about what you left behind or what can go wrong, and get excited about what might be happening right now. Here are some powerful tools to get you back from the past, stop you whizzing ahead into what might be, and appreciate all the magic and wonder that is right slap-bang in front of you now.

Don't be a zombie

We're all prone to being zombies – like when we eat something but hardly remember eating it, let alone what it tasted like. Do you have a drink near you as you read this? If not, go and get one – maybe just a glass of water or a warm cup of tea. Now take that cup, mug, glass or chalice and give it 100 per cent of your attention. I want you to look at that beverage and make sure it's all you're thinking about and focused on, then pick it up. Pay attention to how the glass or cup feels when you hold it in your hand: is it cold, warm, hot? Now raise it to your lips and focus on the very moment that glass or cup touches your lips: does your tongue water in anticipation of what's to come? Can you already picture exactly how the liquid will taste? Now take a sip of that drink and really taste it – I mean savour every single drop. And as you drink it, follow its journey in your mouth, swirling around your teeth, your gums, your tongue, and continue to follow its magical journey down your throat into your tummy.

That, my beautiful friends, is mindfulness. You just learned how to be mindful and to keep yourself in the present. How easy was that? And that's what I mean when I say don't be a zombie. Be more present with everything you do: when you drink, when you eat, when you cuddle your dog, play with your kids, chop a carrot for dinner or walk down the street with the sun on your skin. Feel it; experience the moment with every fibre of your being. No past, no future, just the incredible now that you have not been paying enough attention to thus far.

Be the narrator of the movie of your life

If you find yourself being swallowed up by thoughts of how things used to be or the fear of what's to come, imagine there's a documentary being filmed about you and your day right now. You are the narrator on this incredibly interesting show that will be aired on a leading documentary channel next week. So, if you're in the shower, say out loud, 'I am washing myself clean. I feel invigorated and I smell fresh as a daisy.' If you feel like a complete idiot saying it out loud, then say it to yourself in your head, but don't forget to do it in the dramatic voice of a documentary narrator like David Attenborough: 'I am making a delicious cup of tea... I have turned the kettle on and am excitingly waiting for it to boil so I can soak the teabag and have a warm, cosy cuppa.' By narrating your actions, you are forcing yourself to be in the here and now; you are being present in every action, every moment and every experience.

Catch yourself with a quote

Sometimes awareness is all we need to snap ourselves out of the negative funk we find ourselves in. So, if you find yourself lost in daydreams of the future or romanticizing the life you used to live, have a word, phrase or quote that will remind you to get back to the here and now. Something like:

'I can choose where to stay and I choose to stay present.'

Or:

'If I live in fear of the future because of what happened in my past, I'll end up losing what I have in the present.'

Having a go at this sentence means you can instantly catch and stop yourself when you find your thoughts going back into the past or fast-forwarding into the future.

Find your feet

Yes, I know they're attached to your legs. But when we're stuck in our head, stuck in thoughts of before or after, we tend to disconnect completely from ourselves and where we are in that very moment. But sometimes all it takes is to ask yourself, *Where are my feet?* By simply asking yourself that question, you move your focus away from your thoughts and towards your physical presence in the here and now. You feel your feet on the ground and get a sense of being rooted on a solid foundation, which automatically brings your focus back to the present. (That's a trick I learned from happiness expert Robert Holden – thanks, Robert!) Better still, tap your feet on the floor for 30 seconds. You have 14,000 nerve endings on the bottom of your feet, and waking up all of those little bad boys will shake you out of your head and the stinking thinking of past or future, quicksticks.

Breathe in and out

I know, you're obviously already breathing in and out, but do you ever actually pay attention to your breathing, or do you just take for granted that you're doing it? Bringing your focus to the present moment can be as quick and simple as paying attention to nothing else but the sensation and experience of your breath. Next time you feel overwhelmed by thoughts of the future, or sad and depressed by memories of the past, just pause and start very consciously to breathe in deeply through your nose for five seconds; pause for one second; then breath out through your nose for five seconds, pause again for one and repeat. Do that five times and put 100 per cent of your focus and concentration into this exercise. It's simple, it's easy and it will bring you back to the present wherever you are. All you have to do is remember to do it!

Put down your phone

Your phone can instantly take you away from the present moment. It may seem like harmless fun, but social media is brilliant at keeping you stuck in the past or fantasizing about the future. Scrolling through Facebook and Instagram immediately disconnects us from the here and now; we start mind-numbingly scrolling through images of days gone by or get lost in what other people are doing.

I'm not saying chuck your phone down the toilet, although that's a very tempting thought for the likes of me. I'm telling you to consciously make the decision to reduce the time you spend aimlessly scrolling and pay more attention to where you are and who you are with.

Don't start your day with the news

I live my life by this very important tool, because if I start my day watching or listening to the negative doom and gloom of what's going on in the world, I very quickly start panicking about the future or longing to go back to the days when things were better. I'm not saying you have to be oblivious to what's going on in the world, just that you don't have to start your day being overwhelmed by that sort of information. If you want to give yourself the greatest chance of staying present, start your day from a place of presence. Don't turn on your television or radio and tune in to the news; rather, put on some calming music and be more conscious of where you are.

Stop dwelling in what was or freaking out about the prospect of what might be, and just start being here, loving your life and who you are right now.

How to change your mindset

One of the greatest spiritual teachers who ever walked this planet was the amazing Louise Hay. Louise had a huge impact on the self-help movement – she managed to make spirituality easy to understand and accessible to all, and helped millions of people to truly transform their lives. One of Louise's most famous techniques for healing and for finding true happiness is the use of positive affirmations. Positive affirmations are uplifting statements that you say out loud (or in your head) to help you to reprogram your previous, negative ways of thinking.

When you repeat these affirmations on a daily basis, the statements eventually become your new truth and completely transform your mindset. Positive affirmations change the way you think about yourself and the world around you, making you confident, peaceful and happy from the inside out.

If you want these things, then it's vital you incorporate positive affirmations into your daily life; you need to make this tool as natural to your everyday existence as brushing your teeth. I say affirmations out loud to myself each and every day, without fail, and it's truly had an incredibly positive and deeply profound impact on how I feel about myself.

Below is a list of positive affirmations. Choose three, write them down on several Post-it notes and stick them up all over your house, everywhere and anywhere – on the fridge, in the fridge, next to the toilet paper, by your bed, on the dashboard of your car, you name it. Whenever you see one of these affirmations, say it to yourself out loud, or silently, three times. No matter what, just do it. Trust me, start working with positive affirmations from today, do it every day for a month, and you'll be amazed at how things in your life start shifting positively and profoundly. If you like, focus on three this week and pick another three for next week, and so on. Remember, your spiritual practice is your own, so if these affirmations don't work for you, feel free to go ahead and create your own.

➡ *Every day, my mind, body and soul get healthier and stronger.*

➡ *My Higher Power is guiding, holding and supporting me.*

➡ *I am so loved, and have a life worth living.*

➡ *Fear isn't real, it's just a tool the ego uses to keep me small.*

➡ *I love myself just as I am right now.*

➡ *I am willing to let go of negative thinking.*

➡ *I let go of old beliefs and thoughts that no longer serve me.*

➡ *I see myself through kind and loving eyes.*

➡ *I have a choice. I choose positive thoughts that help me heal.*

➡ *I let go of the past that has gone and the future that doesn't exist.*

➡ *I trust that everything in my life is as it should be right now.*

➡ *My inner light always shines bright.*

➡ *I can achieve anything and everything.*

➡ *I am open to new ways of being, thinking and feeling.*

➡ *I do not stress about things I cannot control.*

➡ *I choose to trust the Universe.*

➡ *I am worthy of the very best in life.*

➡ *I am thankful for the blessings in my life – I find them everywhere.*

➡ *I am in the process of becoming the very best version of myself.*

Remember, you need to say your chosen affirmations to yourself every single day.

'You have the power to heal your life, and you need to know that. We think so often that we are helpless, but we're not. We always have the power of our minds... Claim and consciously use your power.'

LOUISE HAY

CHAPTER 6

What's All This Nonsense about Self-Love?

Cancer has probably been part of your life for so long that you've started believing it's part of your identity and you don't know who you are without it. But you're not cancer, and cancer is most definitely not inextricably linked to who you are. In order for you to truly comprehend and believe this, however, you must first learn to truly love yourself.

Self-love gets such a bad rap nowadays – corny, clichéd and cheesy like a pungent blue cheese. And yes, maybe self-love is a bit cheesy, clichéd and naff – but so what? Who cares how cheesy self-love is if it can dramatically change your life in beautiful and positive ways?

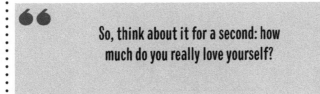

> **So, think about it for a second: how much do you really love yourself?**

The reason this question is so important – perhaps the most important question you can ask yourself – is because truly loving and accepting yourself as you are right now is your Willy Wonka-style golden ticket to happiness and peace. Loving yourself is about feeding and nourishing your soul; loving yourself is the quickest way to heal; loving yourself creates a force field of positivity, love and hope. Want proof? Researcher Masaru Emoto conducted an experiment in which he placed water and rice in three separate jars. Every day for 30 days he would speak out loud to the jars of rice and water. To the first jar he would say, 'Thank you', to the second jar he would say, 'You idiot!' and he completely ignored the third jar. By the end of the 30 days, the jar Emoto had been thanking daily had fermented beautifully; the jar he'd completely ignored had a layer of black mould on the top; and the jar of rice and water he'd insulted was completely black and rotten.*

Imagine yourself as one of those jars of rice. If you neglect yourself – don't listen to your own wants and needs – or if you

---

* 'This Rice Experiment is Proof: The Power of Positivity Alters Our Physical World', *Power of Positivity*, https://www.powerofpositivity.com/scientific-proof-the-power-of-positivity-alters-our-physical-world/ [accessed 3 August 2020]

are constantly putting yourself down and beating yourself up, then your life is going to be mouldy and rotten. But if you start learning how to truly love yourself then your life will reflect that positivity and loving self-regard.

When I finished my treatment, I didn't know what self-love was. I'd spent my life berating myself, never feeling good enough, always beating myself up and putting myself down. I'd struggled with low self-esteem and lack of confidence, and battled with bulimia, anorexia and self-harm. Yes, many women struggle with how they look, many of us have issues about our body shape and weight, but multiply that by a billion and it doesn't come even close to the self-hate and insanity of an eating disorder.

For my whole life prior to cancer, I based my self-worth on my physical appearance, and the two things I prided myself on most were my long, blonde curly hair and my great cleavage. As brutal as it sounds, I believe the only way I was ever going to truly understand self-love and self-acceptance was to have the two things I depended on for my self-worth taken away from me. My left breast was removed and I lost all my beautiful hair. I also put on a lot of weight as a result of all the steroids I had to take during the chemotherapy. Turns out I had to get bald, fat and have a boob removed to learn the most important lesson in my life – but I truly believe there was no other way I was going to learn that lesson. When I received my diagnosis, I didn't care about the illness; I didn't care that I had stage-three cancer and it could kill me. What I cared most about was losing my looks – that I'd be absolutely nothing without them.

My worst fear was presented to me, and I am so grateful that it was because it was the only way I could finally overcome all of my demons.

It took a while for me to realize it, but that constantly chastising and rebuking old self died during my cancer treatment journey. Cancer was my wake-up call. I had the opportunity to reassess my whole life and do things differently. And the key that opened up the door to my new life was learning how to fall in love with myself for the very first time.

No matter how corny and Gorgonzola-smelling you think self-love is, it's also the magic that can create miracles and make you the happiest you've ever been in your whole life.

Loving yourself is how you set yourself free.

I love you. Sincerely, me.

These days, I love me so much. Not in the vain, 'I'm just so damn amazing and better than everyone else' kind of way. No. In the way that I never say a bad word to myself. I don't criticize or put myself down any more. I forgive myself for my mistakes and motivate myself to learn and grow from them. I give and do for myself all the things that make me happy, like rolling around on the floor with my dogs, or making a delicious romantic candlelit dinner just for little old me, myself and beautiful I.

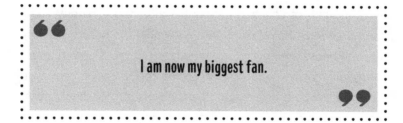

> **I am now my biggest fan.**

I believe in me, I am proud of me and I adore the ground I walk on. And because I feel this way about myself, I no longer get so caught up in negativity, fear, anxiety and all the other stuff that doesn't make my spirit soar.

Learning to love yourself is the easiest way to heal; learning to love yourself is the easiest way to move on from the cancer treatment and live the greatest life you can dream of. By focusing on self-acceptance, self-understanding and self-appreciation, your life transforms and you let go of the negativity without any conscious effort. When you shift the way you think and feel about yourself, everything else in your life naturally and effortlessly shifts alongside you.

When you see something small and vulnerable, like a young child who's grazed their knee or a baby bird that's fallen out of its nest, your natural instinct is to reach out and envelop them in your care, right? Well, now you must do exactly the same to yourself – treat yourself as fragile and vulnerable because you went through a trauma, exactly the same way you would treat that child or baby bird. You deserve the same patience, concern, sympathy, empathy, support, affection, kindness and love. Nothing good will come from giving yourself a hard time, and nothing bad will come from loving and accepting yourself. So which one do you choose?

After the hell of cancer treatment – after those bloody awful chemo needles being stuck into my veins, the poison seeping into my body, the hectic side-effects – I made a commitment to myself that I would never again be the reason for my own suffering. I would never again be the reason I felt down, less-than, anxious or any other negative feeling. I promised myself that from now on I was going to be the one who would lift me up, who would nurture and believe in me more than anybody else. And I would do anything I had to in order to learn how to love myself like that. Self-love isn't an easy thing to accomplish, but if someone like me – who hated herself so profoundly she self-harmed and had an eating disorder – could completely transform to falling head over heels with exactly who she is, then anyone can.

When you look at your reflection in the mirror, what do you see? Someone who is damaged and broken? A victim of disease? Someone who is unattractive and unworthy of unconditional love? Those were just some of the things I would see staring back at me after cancer treatment. In Chapter 5 I explained how Louise Hay introduced me to the power of positive affirmations, and it was Louise Hay, too, who helped me to start the greatest romance of my life – the one with myself. That's why I am going to share another of her greatest exercises – one that will bring about an incredible, positive change in your life and enable you to love yourself from the inside out. This exercise is a prerequisite if you want your life to become one big, fat, juicy, happy miracle. And all you need is a mirror – a hand mirror, your bathroom mirror; any mirror will do.

Let me stress that this exercise is non-negotiable: if you want to fall in love with yourself exactly the way you are, this is, hands down, the best way to do it.

⇨ MIRROR, MIRROR ⇦

I have to admit, when I started incorporating this exercise into my daily routine, after my treatment had finished, I hated every second of it. It felt wrong and disingenuous; like I was lying to myself. There were moments where the exercise would make me cry uncontrollably or just get exceedingly frustrated and angry. But no matter what it brought up for me, I still did it every single day, and I still do it every single day and will continue to do so for the rest of my life, because it has literally transformed the way I feel about myself.

Here's what I want you to do:

Every single morning, before you pick up your toothbrush, pause for a moment and look at yourself in the mirror. I don't mean judge yourself; I don't mean criticize your bed hair or lament the new zit that wasn't on your chin when you went to bed last night. No; I want you to look further than that, past the superficial; I want you to look deep into your eyes and see your soul. Look into your eyes the way you would look at somebody that you really, really love, like your partner, your child, your parent or your pet, then tell yourself – out loud – 'I love you.'

Yes, you read that right, I'm asking you to look in the mirror every morning, lovingly stare back at your reflection and say – out loud:

'I love you, [your name], I really, really love you just as you are right now.'

Yes, you'll feel like a weirdo, and your loved ones might think you've completely lost the plot if they hear you declare undying love to yourself. But what's more important: what other people think or being truly happy?

When you're doing something as monumental as learning to really love yourself for the first time, it's bound to feel weird and uncomfortable at the beginning, but just keep doing it anyway. Louise Hay herself said this exercise isn't easy; but sometimes the miracles come from the challenges, from facing the fear and overcoming it. Sometimes happiness is lying just the other side of fear, and the only way to get to it is to face that fear and walk straight through it.

When I started telling myself 'I love you' in the mirror I didn't believe a word of it. It was nonsense; it made me cringe. I felt completely detached from the person in the mirror, and even more detached from thinking anything nice and loving about myself. Doing it felt so horrible that it would have been easier to just give up. But I wanted to be happy and I was willing to do anything to find that happiness. So, I just kept doing it, until one day, maybe a month after I started the exercise, I suddenly started connecting to the words I was saying to myself and believing them. It was a bloody miracle. I said those words in the mirror just as I had every morning, but one day it felt different – and I felt different. One of the greatest moments of my life was when I realized that, for the very first time in my existence, I really did love myself.

But it wasn't really the first time I'd felt that way. We all felt that way about ourselves at the beginning, in early infancy. As babies we are mesmerized by our reflection in the mirror; we gaze at ourselves in wonder and amazement and grin from ear to ear when we see how awesome and beautiful we are. But years of conditioning make us forget that loving relationship we had with ourselves at the very start of our lives. Family attitudes, peer pressure, trying to fit in and be liked – it all took a toll on us until we lost that self-love altogether and forgot it was ever there.

So, essentially, what I'm asking you to do is to remember. I'm not expecting you to instantly start loving yourself, but I am asking you to remain open to the possibility and keep trying, because eventually something deep inside you will reconnect and remember that pure self-love you once had.

Get your priorities right

I'd like you to get a piece of paper and a pen, and write down the five most important people in your life.

Yes – right now, please.

Now, I don't need to see your list to already know that there's a 99.9 per cent chance you got it wrong. Don't worry – when I wrote my list for the first time, I got it wrong too. That's the point: we've all been getting it wrong. But you're about to learn one the biggest lessons in your life and take one of the most important first steps towards a life of unconditionally loving yourself.

Try the exercise again – write a list of the five most important people in your life – but this time start with your own name at the very top of your list, as number one.

YOU are the most important person in your life.

YOU are number one.

YOU should always be at the top of your list of priorities.

That's not selfish, that's called self-love and it will not only transform your life but also transform your relationships with every other person on your list and every other person in your life.

Learning to truly love yourself involves changing old beliefs and behaviours, which up until now may have felt part of your DNA and 100 per cent valid. For example, that putting other people's happiness before your own is a noble and loving thing to do. Wrong! Sacrificing your own wellbeing for others is *not* the right thing to do, because if you yourself aren't happy then the people you love pick up on that, and they're not happy either.

It is easy to get bogged down by the craziness of every day, to get focused on everyone else around you and push your own needs aside. But when you do this, not only do you suffer, you are also not at your best for everyone else around you.

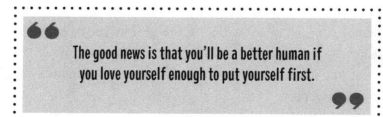

The good news is that you'll be a better human if you love yourself enough to put yourself first.

When you're on a plane, what does the safety card say? What does the air hostess always stress when showing you emergency procedures? *Put on your own life vest and oxygen mask first before helping others with theirs.* If you want to be truly helpful, caring, supportive and nurturing to others, you first have to take care of yourself and your own needs. We're constantly adapting to the wants and needs of those we love, but given that we were diagnosed with cancer and went through the hell of treatment, shouldn't we be making our own wellbeing and happiness important too?

I am not embarrassed or ashamed to admit that I'm the most important person in my life. I will always be first in my life and everyone else will always be second. That may sound brutal and selfish but it's actually the opposite. We've been brainwashed to believe that if you want to consider yourself a truly good person then you must self-sacrifice all the time. Pardon my language, but f**k that. Self-sacrifice makes you frustrated, tense, anxious, annoyed, tired, resentful and angry. How exactly does that make you a good person and helpful to others? It doesn't.

I really don't care how good a person you claim to be, because if you don't have your own s**t together then you're no good to anyone else. However, if you prioritize your own wants and needs, give yourself the quiet time your soul craves, nourish yourself the way your body longs for and support yourself the way your heart wants, then, and only then, can you truly be the most helpful to others. This doesn't mean you suddenly shouldn't care about your children, your spouse, your friends or work colleagues. It just means you shouldn't care about them more than you care about yourself.

Putting yourself first will positively impact everyone around you. Ever since I started making myself my top priority, my relationships all transformed into healthy connections with healthy communication. The happier I made myself, the happier those around me became, too.

Take it from me: it's totally OK and acceptable to be self-loving and make yourself your number one. Put on your own oxygen mask and life vest first and you will learn not only to love yourself, but to love everyone else better.

How to love yourself

There's a vast array of tools and exercises you can incorporate into your day-to-day life to reprogram your feelings, thoughts and beliefs about yourself. So, if you want to experience the freedom and joy of self-acceptance, self-forgiveness, self-kindness and self-love then roll up your sleeves and prepare to get your hands dirty (metaphorically speaking). I don't care if you feel like a giant idiot or that all this self-love malarkey reaches Roquefort levels of cheesiness. Do it anyway, because just reading this book isn't enough – there needs to be some action involved too.

Self-love means accepting yourself for who you are right now, with all your beautiful frailties, faults and imperfections. So, yes, maybe you have damaged breasts or a colostomy bag; maybe your hair is thinning or you're completely bald; maybe you have some crap side-effects from the medication you're on and feel like a lethargic, lazy lump. It doesn't matter – you must learn to love yourself unconditionally, despite it all.

You must learn to love the good, the bad, the damaged, the ugly, the beautiful, the mistakes, the accomplishments, the fragility, the strength – all of it. You can't just pick the bits to love and despise the rest – that, my friend, is not how the art of self-love works.

Self-love is radical self-acceptance, and I promise that if you can nail this concept then the negativity you've been feeling will evaporate all by itself – poof! The pain, negativity and struggle will disappear in a puff of magical smoke if you can learn to master the art of true self-love.

Below are some powerful ways to get you tripping, tumbling, somersaulting and falling madly in love with yourself. You don't have to do them all, but I would suggest you give each one a go before deciding which ones resonate with you and which don't. (And remember to keep up your mirror work – that bit is mandatory.)

1. **Don't treat life as a competition**

    Love yourself enough not to compare your insides to everyone else's outsides. Just because another cancer survivor posts that they've just finished a triathlon in record-breaking time, it doesn't mean their recovery is any quicker or better than yours. Just because the hair of the person you sat next to during chemo is growing back twice as fast as yours, it doesn't mean they're any more beautiful than you are. Life is not a competition.

    From now on, every time you feel envy or jealousy creeping up on you; any time you start comparing yourself with, or feeling less than, somebody else, I want you to imagine saying to them: 'Good for you!' How exactly is that self-loving? Simple: by spreading love and positivity to others, you attract love and positivity to yourself. If you dwell on comparison, resentment, jealousy and envy, you'll just attract the same negativity towards yourself. It isn't rocket science – like attracts like. If you feel happy for someone then happiness will be drawn to you; if you believe someone is deserving of their good luck and fortune, the Universe will find you deserving of abundance and prosperity too.

So, show how much you love yourself by sending out positive vibes to the people you envy or compare yourself to.

2. **Connect with people – and not only online!**

Spend less time scrolling through social media and more time genuinely reaching out to people. I don't mean sliding them a DM or a sending a virtual greeting card to their inbox. I mean actually picking up the phone, finding the time in your day to reach out and ask somebody how they are and actually paying attention to the answer. We're stuck with ourselves all the time, with the thoughts that race around our brains at 10,000 mph, with our feelings, with our daily dramas and our ongoing struggles. But by thinking about someone else, authentically listening to and connecting with another person, you focus less on all your own strife and struggles. You get a break from you.

Remember that listening to a friend doesn't mean that you take whatever they've said and make it about you. Let's be honest: most of us don't listen. Most of the time we nod our heads and are either lost in thought or wondering how we can make ourselves the subject of what the other person is saying. But taking over the conversation, or making their stuff about your stuff, completely defeats the purpose. I'm asking you to authentically listen to someone else, to focus on the other person's agenda, to really step outside of yourself and make it all about that other person. That, my friends, is a sacred art.

3. **Celebrate everything about yourself**

We're so quick to belittle ourselves when we don't succeed, when we're not being good enough, happy enough or successful enough. But self-love doesn't have space for that kind of attitude towards ourselves. Self-love is about celebrating what we get right, not picking ourselves apart for what we get wrong. Self-love is about focusing on the achievements, no matter how teeny-tiny they may seem.

Maybe you haven't had the energy to exercise since finishing treatment but today you managed to do the ten-minute walk to drop the kids at school, or to walk around the block, or do a five-minute yoga routine in bed. And if you're trying to live a healthier lifestyle and cut down on refined sugar, don't beat yourself up because you had a cupcake before bed last night. Instead, focus on the fact you had yoghurt with fresh fruit for breakfast when you could have chosen a Danish pastry. Be proud of yourself for what you managed to do; don't berate yourself for not doing more. All you can do is your best, and your best will always be enough.

It's about progress, not perfection. It's about being out there in the big wide world, doing the best we can with what we've got. We went through cancer treatment, for f**k's sake, so how about we start celebrating who we are and stop beating ourselves up? I choose to celebrate me and my achievements, no matter how small or seemingly insignificant they may seem – like managing to sleep a whole night without being woken up by a hot flush or a cold sweat, choosing to have a salad with my burger instead of fries, going a whole 24 hours without thinking about the cancer coming back, or enjoying dinner with friends without once mentioning the word cancer!

So, buy an organic, sugar-free cupcake, stick a candle in it, light it up and shout a loud 'Well done me!' then blow out the candle and make a wish. Celebrate the awesomeness of who you are every day. You've been beating yourself up for long enough. Now you're going to spend the rest of your life making it up to yourself.

4. Let yourself say no

I used to think being a good person meant always saying yes to people, whether I wanted to or not. And if I didn't say yes, that meant I was a self-centred asshole. But I couldn't have been more wrong. Sometimes we do too much for other people, to our own detriment; we want to please other people so much that we stretch ourselves too thin and forget to look after ourselves. As we saw earlier in this chapter, only if you take care of yourself, if you make sure your needs are met first, can you be the best version of yourself and offer the best parts of yourself to others.

For example, agreeing to go to a party I really don't want to go to, just to please a friend who needs a wing-woman by her side, is not a good idea. I'd be going to that party out of obligation and under duress, and spend the whole evening secretly wishing I was at home with my dogs and resenting my friend for 'forcing' me to be out. But that's the thing: she wouldn't have 'forced' me to go to the party at all; at least, I'm pretty certain she wouldn't have had a gun to my head blackmailing me to be her plus-one. No, only I would be putting that guilt and pressure on myself; the ego would whisper what a terrible friend I'd be if I didn't put on a little black dress, drink overpriced cocktails all night and have a stinking hangover in the morning. Well, I'm sorry, ego, but I went through cancer treatment and it sucked, so I'm not forcing myself to do things that suck any more.

If, at the core of you and deep in your heart, you really don't want to do something, then be very loving to yourself about it and just say no. Learning to love myself by saying no (with loving kindness) to others changed so much for me. It alleviated my feelings of obligation, of dread, of anxiety and resentment. I had so much more respect for myself when I stopped giving in to other people's demands all the time. I'm not saying I became a selfish bugger and did only what suited me. There are times when your loved ones need you, when there's something really important to them and you get involved because your heart tells you to. But that's the difference – doing it from a heartspace instead of being guilted into it by the voice of the ego.

So, next time you're about to say yes to somebody, just take a moment. Feel the reasons you're saying yes. Is it because it will bring you genuine joy? Is it coming from a place of pure love because you know how much it means to that person? Or are you saying yes out of guilt, obligation or fear that those people won't like you any more if you set boundaries? Stop saying yes to everyone and this alone will change your life.

5. **Seek your own approval**

    As you start loving yourself more, there may be people who dig you less. But hey, you're never gonna get the whole world to love you. You can become the juiciest, most loving, most spiritual and kindest human being on the planet and there will still be people who just don't like you very much. And that's OK, because you're not living your life to get other people's approval. You need to be able to look in the mirror and like the person you see smiling back at you. As long as you know that your 'no' boundaries are coming from a pure and unselfish place, then that is all that matters.

    Nowadays I am surrounded by people who uplift, respect and approve of me just as I am, with my healthy boundaries and my ability to say no. In fact, I've inspired a lot of my loved ones to do the same, to the point where they've even started saying no to me!

6. **Avoid running on empty**

    I don't know about you, but when I'm feeling tired I turn into Oscar the Grouch from *Sesame Street*. I start snapping at everyone, I cry at the drop of a hat, I hate myself for no reason whatsoever and start hating everything and everyone around me, too. Not a good look and not how I want to be.

Yes, I know we're all busy, we have commitments we must attend to such as kids, jobs, shopping, and so on. But if you ignore how tired you're feeling, then you start running on a low battery and this both compromises your ability to get things done properly and impacts your capacity to cope. So, if you're tired, acknowledge it and have a rest, because this is critical to staying healthy physically, mentally, emotionally and spiritually. Simply by having an early night or allowing yourself a nap for an hour during the day, you can instantly rejuvenate and change the way you feel. Sometimes loving yourself is as simple as giving yourself a break.

The above are all great tactics for developing self-love but there are plenty more out there, so feel free to explore and discover new ways to be kinder and more loving to yourself.

Time for romance

Why is it that romance is something we only do for, or with, somebody else?

You don't need anybody else to be romantic. You can enjoy romance right now, because self-love means 'romancing yourself'. It means making yourself feel loved and utterly wonderful. You don't need someone else to take you up to cloud nine, you can get up there all by yourself. You don't have to wait for Valentine's Day for someone to buy you your favourite chocolates from that expensive speciality shop down the road. You can be romantic any day of the year you want: go to that speciality shop today and buy those chocolates that make your tongue melt, your toes curl and your heart tingle. Go home, run a hot bath with lots of bubbles, light some candles, play some sexy music and eat those chocolates while you're luxuriously soaking yourself. Even better, have a glass of champagne at the same time.

Why do all this? Because it's romantic, and you're falling in love with you, so you need to woo yourself and whisk yourself off your feet. Self-romance should become as normal and natural as doing something kind and loving for your kids, your partner or a friend.

I'm not saying you have to be all Walt Disney with yourself every day, but you do have to be a little bit Walt Disney with yourself at least once a week. Whether that's singing to the birds in your garden while throwing them breadcrumbs, putting on your poshest frock or tuxedo and dancing to that cheesy song you secretly love more than any other, eating a box of chocolates in the bath, having dessert as a starter or wearing edible technicolour rainbow undies that no one else will see. The point is to get gooey with yourself, to stop expecting someone else to woo you and to start doing it yourself.

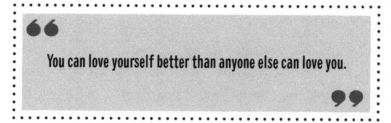

You can love yourself better than anyone else can love you.

Think back to one of your first childhood crushes. Picture the person who made you feel as though you might spontaneously combust into flowers, rainbows and unicorns just because they'd smiled in your direction. Try to remember that feeling – as though your heart was about to burst out of your chest every time you saw them. Now, if you wanted to dazzle that person, if you wanted to charm them, win their heart, make their soul do a somersault and make them smile from ear to ear, what would you do? Whatever you think of is exactly what you should be doing for yourself.

How to seduce yourself

Here are some ideas to tickle yourself pink, blow yourself away and to trip, slip and make yourself fall madly in love with you. (None of these suggestions are gender-biased, so none of you have an excuse not to go for it.)

Body cream

During a sexy and romantic evening with someone, if you were to rub body lotion onto their skin you'd do it slowly, seductively and sensually. If you rubbed cream onto a baby or small child, you'd do it very consciously and sensitively, with loving care. But when we put cream on ourselves, we just slop it on, rub it in and get dressed. WTF is that about? Now, every time I put cream on my skin, I take my time and I do it with love. I caress my skin; I focus all my attention on what I'm doing and I moisturize my body in a loving way. I don't rush it just because it's my body and not someone else's – that's just ludicrous. We should be as delicate, patient and kind to our own skin as we would be when rubbing body lotion onto somebody else's.

Flowers

Newsflash: you don't have to wait for anyone else to buy flowers for you. Amazing, right? In fact, it's even better when you buy yourself flowers because you get to pick the ones you want, instead of the crusty chrysanthemums someone gives you from the local petrol station. I want you to go to a proper florist's shop and take your time; wander around, marvel at all the beauty, smell the flowers, touch the petals, take in all the colours and shapes, and choose the ones that most appeal to you. Then treat yourself to those flowers. Take them home and put them in a vase by your bed, and I guarantee that, every time you look at those flowers, they make you smile and warm your heart.

Breakfast in bed

For those of you who have a family, you may be waiting for your next birthday before you get treated to breakfast in bed. And for the single crew out there, including me – well, my dogs are awesome but not awesome enough to prepare me something delicious and bring it to my bed on a tray. So, why don't we bring ourselves breakfast in bed? If you have a family then by all means make breakfast for them first, but then put yours on a tray and go back to bed to eat it. If you live alone, make something yummy then hop back into bed and enjoy breakfast snuggled under the covers while reading a book.

Flirting with yourself

Look in the mirror and tell yourself how damn sexy you are; that you've never seen eyes as beautiful; or how stylish you look in those baggy pyjama bottoms and old, faded T-shirt. Yes, you might feel like a bit of a knob, but then lovingly laugh at yourself – giggle as though someone totally gorgeous just gave you a compliment, and you're all embarrassed and don't know what to say.

Love letters

When I'm in a relationship, I love leaving little notes for my beloved to find in unexpected places – a bedside drawer, the glove compartment of their car, on the fridge, in the freezer. But now I leave love notes for myself to find. Stuff like:

➡ *I'm so incredibly proud of you.*

➡ *I love you so much.*

➡ *Your ass looks great today.*

➡ *I believe in you. Go out there and dazzle the world with your beautiful light.*

➡ *You're a rock star. Own it.*

It helps that I have the worst memory in the world, because I forget where the notes are and then genuinely get a surprise when I find one. So, cut up some paper, write at least 20 secret sweet nothings, then hide them all over your home for you to find at a later time.

Pamper yourself

Book yourself in for a body massage (or a ten-minute head massage), a manicure or a facial – any kind of pampering treatment that isn't essential but will make you feel sublime and sexy afterwards.

Date night

Take yourself to see a movie, even better if it's in the middle of the day because that's extra-naughty and extra-romantic. And don't go to a film you think you ought to see just because it's indie and cool or because everyone else is going to see it. Go and see a guilty-pleasure movie and don't invite anyone else to go with you. Yes, it might seem scary, but a first date always is. So, allow yourself to feel nervous, to have the butterflies, but go and see that cheesy movie on your lonesome nevertheless, and stuff your face with popcorn while you're watching it. If sitting in a quiet, dark cinema by yourself is too much, then how about taking yourself on a date to an exhibition or a museum? Most of them offer guided tours on headphones, so you don't even have to feel silly walking around alone.

Spoil yourself

Go to your local snazzy deli and buy yourself a mini bottle of champagne, some artisan chocolates or some posh Spanish smoked almonds. Or take yourself to a local street market and make a pact with yourself to buy something for less than £20 that makes your heart and face smile. Be generous to yourself materially, once in a while; don't wait for someone else to buy you a present. If you've had your eye on a gorgeous pair of earrings, buy them, and someone else can always buy you the matching necklace or ring another time.

You've got mail

Find a little time to sit down and write yourself a letter that will give you a boost next time you're feeling down in the dumps. Imagine that someone you love very deeply is going through a hard time – perhaps a relationship hasn't worked out or they're having trouble at work. Think of the loving things you would want to say to uplift them, to inspire them and make them feel wonderful about themselves, and then put those words into a letter to yourself. Write the sort of kind, reassuring and supportive things to yourself that you would love to be able to read when you're having a bad day. You need to know that someone has your back, and that someone is you.

Once you've written the letter, pop it into an envelope, put your address and a stamp on it, and post it. When you receive the letter in a few days' time, don't open it. Remember that you wrote it for when you're going through a particularly bad time, so put the letter away somewhere safe and, next time you feel down in the dumps, make yourself a cup of tea, curl up on the sofa and read that letter out loud to yourself.

Say sorry and accept your apology

If a loved one makes a mistake or does something that hurts you, hopefully they apologize and try to make things right. And hopefully you're loving enough to accept their apology and put the whole thing behind you. I suggest you start doing the same for yourself.

The fact is, I often make mistakes; the only difference now is that I don't spend the foreseeable future making myself feel guilty and ashamed of it. That's not to say I give myself permission to screw up, but when I do screw up, I sincerely say sorry to myself and I accept my apology. I give myself permission to be human and to make mistakes.

Saying sorry isn't something you do just for other people. If you make a mistake and you suffer as a consequence, you need to apologize to yourself just as you would if the mistake affected anyone else. You deserve to give yourself the same respect. Maybe you haven't taken yourself to the gym all week and you're feeling crap about it. Say to yourself something along the lines of 'I'm sorry, me, I know I should have gone to the gym and done some exercise this week, but I just wasn't in the mood. I'm really sorry if I made you feel like a lazy lump, but how about we go for a nice leisurely stroll in the park?' Then accept your apology and don't punish yourself. You apologized, so forgive yourself. Go for that leisurely walk and breathe in some sweet-smelling fresh air.

These are just a few ideas of how to romance yourself and be more loving to yourself, but no one knows you better than you do, so take your time and think about what would really make you swoon and go weak at the knees. What would make you go all floppy, gaga, silly and giggly? Whatever those things are, you need to be regularly doing them for yourself.

CHAPTER 7

Coping with Cancer's After-Effects

There are so many after-effects following cancer treatment: the physical after-effects of the chemotherapy, radiation or any other procedures you might have had; the side-effects from medication that you were taking or quite possibly still are; and the psychological after-effects, such as the fear of death or of the cancer returning. I wish I had the answers to get rid of these things for you altogether, but in this chapter I'll be offering you suggestions on how to at least manage and cope with them.

What if the cancer comes back?

My oncologist was very honest when she told me it was likely I was going to eventually die with, or from, cancer. But I am free from fear. I no longer worry about when the cancer will come back; in fact I hardly even think about it any more.

That doesn't mean I just clicked my fingers and the fear disappeared. I used to be crippled by the fear that my cancer would return or that it had never left my body and no one had spotted it. If I got an ache in my finger, I thought it was cancer. If I got a sore throat or my eye twitched, I thought it was cancer.

But being consumed by that kind of fear is no way to live. Whether you're in remission from cancer or still living with it, the fact is you're still here. You're alive and you can't waste your life by constantly being afraid.

I know I've already told you this but, just in case you're still struggling to believe me, I'll tell you again: fear is an illusion created by the ego to keep control over you. The more scared you are, the more you curl up in a little ball and hide from the beauty and potential of your life, the more the ego thrives. The fear you are feeling is the ego stealing your power. All you have to do is make the decision to take your power back.

> 'I learned that courage was not the absence of fear, but the triumph over it. The brave man is not he who does not feel afraid, but he who conquers that fear.'
>
> NELSON MANDELA, *LONG WALK TO FREEDOM*

Don't get me wrong: not all fear is bad and not all of it comes from the ego. There's good fear, too – the fear you feel from your heart that's a message from your soul. The kind of fear you get when a big grizzly bear is charging right at you and you start running for your life. That kind of fear doesn't emanate from your thoughts, from your mind or from your head, where the ego resides. That kind of healthy, good, keep-you-safe kind of fear comes from your heart and soul. But the fear of cancer coming back (or, if you have an incurable cancer, the fear of it taking your life from you) is not that heartfelt fear – it's the fear that happens when the ego takes over your thoughts and runs riot with them. Your freedom lies in knowing the difference.

So next time you feel fear of any kind, try to tap into its source. Is the fear coming from your head? From your thoughts? Or is the fear a feeling in your heart, that's coming from your soul? If you feel the fear of cancer, immediately say some affirmations out loud so the ego can hear that you're not falling for its tricks any more. For example, you could say:

➡ *This fear is an illusion and I will not believe it any more.*

➡ *Nothing will hold me back from living my greatest life.*

➡ *I am fearless and brave.*

➡ *The ego cannot and will not stand in my way.*

➡ *I have nothing to fear because my Higher Power is protecting me.*

➡ *I am willing to release all thought-based fear.*

It's all about affirmative action; when you feel the tickle of fear, do something that will stop it dead in its tracks, anything at all that involves kicking the ego and its fake fear right in the ass.

Remember, every day is a new chapter, with new possibilities and the opportunity to do things differently, so today could be the day that you decide you'll no longer allow the ego to control your life with fear.

⇨ FEAR EMERGENCY ⇦

I use this exercise whenever fear blindsides me; it's incredibly soothing and fast-working. I use it as soon as I feel overwhelmed by fear or anxiety, and it quickly helps me to calm down and gain perspective.

1. Find somewhere quiet and private where you'll be undisturbed for five minutes.

2. Stand up straight and take five long, deep breaths in and out.

3. Focus on where in your body you're feeling the fear. The fear thoughts are coming from your head, but they may manifest in other areas in your body. For example, when I get overcome with ego fear, I get a horrible hollow and empty feeling in my stomach. Perhaps you feel the fear as a fogginess in your head or tightness in your chest. Just locate where the fear is for you.

4. Now focus on that place the fear is coming from and picture what that fear looks like, just like you did when you gave a face to the ego. My fear is usually a big black blob like sticky, thick tar. Yours might be a dark, black shadow, green slime or a heavy jagged rock – whatever resonates with you.

5. Now pull that fear out of your body. Yes, literally, with your hands: let go of being self-conscious and physically act out pulling this fear from wherever it's hiding. If you imagined the fear as a black

shadow in your head, imagine pulling that black shadow out of your ear. If it was an evil goblin lodged in your throat, open your mouth and pull that little bugger out of you. Now hold the fear tight in your hands so it can't get away. (I know this all sounds nutty but just go along with me, please, because it may just work for you.)

6. With your imaginary fear-object cupped in your hands, start vigorously rubbing your hands together as fast and hard as you can, with vigour and determination. By doing this, you are transforming that negative fear into positive energy. Imagine the fear between your hands dissolving into a warm energy that's so bright its light starts seeping between your fingers.

7. Now stop rubbing your hands together and slowly pull them apart so that they're parallel to each other. Feel the heat of the positive force you created between your palms and imagine that bright, warm, golden light. Feel this light energy pulsating between your hands.

8. Now carefully put this positive light-energy back inside your body, into the hole you left when you pulled the fear out of you. So, if the fear was in your belly, I want you to press your hands against your stomach and imagine the positive energy, the light, penetrating your skin and filling that space with warm, safe, positive vibes.

9. Now take five more deep breaths in and out, and see how you feel.

As insane as this exercise may seem, it saves me every single time I feel extreme fear. The imagination is such an incredibly powerful tool for self-healing, so don't be afraid to use it.

Body image after cancer

The experience of hair loss combined with the deformity of a mastectomy and weight gain from the steroids during chemo was unbearable for me. In fact, when I was at the peak of my treatment, I covered up all the mirrors in my home because my reflection horrified me so much. But the way I felt wasn't due to the cancer; it came down to my lack of self-love. I had no self-compassion or self-acceptance, and as a consequence I was unbelievably cruel to myself.

Not in a million years would I make anyone else feel that way, like they were a monster. If anyone else was bald and bloated from cancer treatment, I wouldn't refuse to look at them; I wouldn't turn away in disgust because of their appearance. So why was I okay with treating myself like that? We willingly do things to ourselves, think things of ourselves and feel things about ourselves, that we wouldn't dare to do, think or feel towards another person.

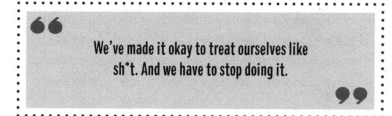

> **We've made it okay to treat ourselves like sh*t. And we have to stop doing it.**

I wish I could go back and apologize to myself, to that girl who was feeling so ugly and broken and just needed some love and acceptance. She reached out to me and I turned my back on her. I will never ever do that to myself again. And I ask you not to do that to yourself, either.

I love my body now. No, really. I love my body even though I have wonky boobs and only one nipple. I love my body even with the parts that are starting to sag. And I'll continue to love my body, whether it's firm or floppy, tanned or pale, hairy or silky smooth, having a hot flush or a cold sweat, bald or bushy, bloated, spotty, dry, oily – whatever.

So how did I start loving my body? Well, to start with I did the mirror exercise I shared with you in Chapter 6: I said I love you to myself in the mirror every single day until it became my truth. And all these years later there's not a single morning when I don't look at my reflection and say to myself, 'I love you, Saskia. I really, love you. Just as you are right now, I love you.' It's a non-negotiable part of my life because it's this commitment to myself that allowed me to transform how I feel about myself and my physical appearance.

Also, I wrote a love letter to my body in which I apologized for being such a b*tch to it. And that's what I'd like you to do now.

⇨ AN APOLOGY TO YOUR BODY ⇦

Find some quiet time to sit and write a heartfelt love letter to your body, apologizing for all the wrongdoings you've inflicted on it. You may not have been as hard on your body as I was, but I'm sure you've still got some making up to do.

Below are the things I apologized for. Not all of them will resonate with you so just pick the ones that you connect with or recall any others you've berated yourself about.

I apologized to my body for:

➡ Continually comparing my body to the bodies of other people, including magazine models and everyone on social media

➡ My never-ending quest for a body that was better, thinner, stronger, leaner, taller, shapelier and generally anything other than the body I was blessed with

➡ Looking at my reflection and constantly critiquing the body I saw in front of me

➡ Telling my body it was fat, ugly, broken, deformed, flabby, scrawny and so on

➡ Forcing my body to overwork itself with exercise when it was tired and just wanted to rest

➡ Not bothering to give my body exercise and attention when it needed and deserved it

➡ Stuffing my body with food I knew wasn't good for it by allowing the ego to hoodwink me into believing it would make me feel better

➡ Skipping meals because fitting into my skinny jeans was more important that nourishing my body and giving it the energy it needed

I want you to apologize to your body for a lifetime of unkindness, but most of all I want you to apologize to your body if you've not accepted and loved it, however it feels and looks, after surviving cancer treatment. In your letter, tell your body how much you love it and how you're going to spend the rest of your life in this big, beautiful world adoring your body, nurturing and nourishing it as best you know how. Then, thank your body for everything it does for you and the things it has always done but you've taken for granted – for giving you a beautiful smile, for always getting you from A to B, for the tingles you get when the sun kisses your skin, the colour of your eyes or your less-than-perfect biceps. Tell your body it's truly beautiful right now, not that it's going to be beautiful once you've shed ten pounds, had reconstruction or got a tan on holiday. And tell it that no matter what happens, going forward, you will love and accept your appearance exactly the way it is, with all its flaws, defects, scars, bumps and lumps.

Don't just read what I'm telling you to do, do it – write the letter. Don't you think your body deserves it?

Living with side-effects

It can take time to recover from the side-effects of cancer treatment or medication. Some side-effects go away quickly, others can take weeks, months or even years to improve; some may even be permanent. Your body will cope with the treatment and recovery in its own way, so it's imperative that you remain kind, patient and accepting of yourself. The bad news is that a lot of the time there isn't much you can actually do about the side-effects. You're alive and this is what you've got to deal with.

> **The good news is that you get to choose your attitude to living with the side-effects.**

Almost eight years later, I still have side-effects from the treatment and from the medication I continue to take. I do what I can to ease the discomfort. For example, for the hot flushes, I always carry a mini electric fan, whatever the season. Yes, I may look slightly odd sitting in a vest top on the train in the depths of winter, fanning myself while everyone else is huddled up in woolly hats and scarves. But I'm okay with that now, because I chose to make peace with this situation and to deliberately switch the direction of my focus to all the good that's going on for me. I'm here, I'm alive and I'm grateful.

I'm not saying you just have to suck it up; I feel for you, and you have my full sympathy for whatever side-effects you're suffering. What I am saying is that the more you focus on the discomfort, the more your life will revolve around that discomfort. If you're feeling self-pity, resentment, annoyance, anger or are just plain fed up with all the side-effects of treatment, you'll be sending out a whole lot of negative energy into the Universe. The Universe is extremely sensitive to our vibrations and it responds accordingly, which means that whatever thoughts and feelings you're focused on, the Universe will focus on too. So, if you spend too much time thinking about how crappy your life is because your joints ache all the time, the Universe won't pick up on the good or bad nature of that, just that your life revolves around these joint pains – so that's what the Universe will focus on, too.

This may all sound like doom and gloom but it's not. What I'm talking about here is the Law of Attraction, and you can use it to radically change your life simply by changing your thoughts and feelings. The Law of Attraction is, quite simply, the idea that our positive or negative thoughts and feelings will manifest positive or negative experiences in our lives; that we will inevitably create more of whatever we think and feel. So, if you spend too much time lamenting and moaning about joint pain, hot flushes or chronic fatigue, the Universe is going to hear the moaning and lamenting and just give you more to moan and lament about. You are a magnet, and therefore you have the choice of what to magnetize into your life. If you focus on the negatives, you draw in negativity; if you focus on the positives you draw in positivity.

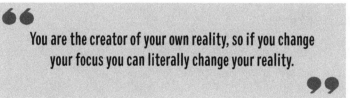

> 66
> **You are the creator of your own reality, so if you change your focus you can literally change your reality.**
> 99

Sounds way too easy to be true, right? That's certainly what I thought when I was first introduced to the concept. When I started trying out this whole Law of Attraction thing, I thought it was a load of rubbish, that there was no way some positive thinking could make my aches, pains and hot flushes subside. But the side-effects didn't seem to be going away anytime soon so I figured I'd give it a go as I had nothing to lose. Whenever I got hit by a hot flush or joints pain, I would try my hardest to focus on something else that was positive, and to send out vibes. Instead of allowing myself to get hot (literally) and bothered, and overwhelmed, I would deliberately distract myself by focusing my attention on something that made me feel happy, such as how much my hair had grown or how lucky I was to have such great friends in my life – anything and everything positive I could think of to stop focusing on the crappiness.

Before learning about the Law of Attraction, whenever I got an overpowering hot flush the following thoughts would fill my head:

I can't bear this – I'm sweating like a pig. I feel like I'm going to spontaneously combust, and my insides are going to splatter all over the walls like a volcano erupting hot, molten lava. It's not fair. Why did I get cancer? Why do I have to go through this every day? Is this going to be my life for ever?

But now I'm like:

Oh, I'm having a hot flush. And then I immediately make myself focus on something else that's really positive.

And guess what? It works. The less I dwell on the negatives in my life, like the physical struggles from the treatment and medication, the less overpowering they are.

Maybe you're struggling with extreme fatigue and find it hard just to get out of bed and make a cup of tea in the morning. Instead of focusing on the struggle, you could choose to focus on how delicious that cup of tea is going to be when you finally do manage to make it. By focusing on the deliciousness and sweetness of the tea, you invite the Universe to bring more deliciousness and sweetness into your life. If you suffer from joint pain (as I still do), you could choose to dwell on the frustration of that – or you could focus on the fact that for the first time in months you managed to walk to the shops and back with no pain at all. In response to your gratitude for the moments you feel pain-free, the Universe will bring you more pain-free things to be grateful for.

Do you see what I'm saying? You'll attract into your life whatever you focus on, so all you need to do is tweak your focus a little bit. Your job is to make sure you try your very best to spend the majority of your day sending out thoughts and feelings that resonate with what you want to be feeling, thinking and experiencing.

It's okay (and perfectly normal) if you don't think positively every waking hour – remember, it's about progress, not perfection, and we're not giving ourselves a hard time any more. Just do the best you can, because your best is always good enough.

By making the choice to keep trying to focus on the positive, I now easily manage to cope with the after-effects of treatment and the side-effects of my medication. But if I hadn't put in the effort to try to think things differently, then those aches and pains would continue to dominate my life.

In Chapter 8 I'll be giving you some tools to help you put the Law of Attraction into practice. If you start incorporating these tools into your life, your struggle with after-effects will get easier.

Love life and cancer

Let's be honest: romantic relationships are hard enough to maintain as it is, without throwing cancer into the mix. Whether you're married, in a relationship or single, going through cancer means you may have to face all kinds of issues in the romantic realm that most other people don't have to deal with. It could be the physical side-effects of the medication or cancer treatment, or feeling uncomfortable with your body post-surgery. What's most important is that you know it's completely normal if your love life is different from how it used to be.

Don't be ashamed of any of the issues you might be facing, or sweep them under the carpet because they're awkward to deal with. The only way past these difficulties is to acknowledge them and get the help you need. Yes, that sucks, because it's uncomfortable and we'd much prefer to listen to the ego telling us to keep quiet and keep our problems to ourselves. But that method doesn't work.

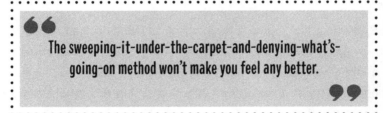

The sweeping-it-under-the-carpet-and-denying-what's-going-on method won't make you feel any better.

It's imperative that you learn to accept and love yourself just as you are, even if your sex drive has left the building, you feel like you just want to detach from others and be alone or you don't want to be held or touched in the way you used to.

If you're in a relationship and you truly love each other, you can work through anything. There are incredible couples' therapists out there who can help you overcome these issues together, because that's exactly what they're trained to do. So, don't try to cope with such serious stuff on your own. Reach out and get the help and guidance that you need, because you're so worthy and deserving of that.

As for the single crew out there, I know what it can be like. I was terrified to start dating for a long time after treatment. I felt broken, like damaged goods on the supermarket shelf that no one would want. When my friends and loved ones urged me to venture out into the dating world, I point-blank refused. They lovingly suggested I sign up to one of the various dating apps, but what was I supposed to write in my bio? 'I love dogs, walks in the forest and have wonky tits because I went through breast cancer'? It felt as though that little piece of information had changed everything, and that as soon as I told a potential suitor about my cancer, they would run a mile.

But that wasn't a genuine reason for not getting out there again. That was me projecting my fears and insecurities onto every single man in the world. In hindsight, I laugh at my audacity, claiming to know how every single man would feel or think about me having been through cancer. I mean, seriously, who did I think I was, a clairvoyant able to read the minds of every single man on the planet?

Eventually, when I was ready, I did get out there and start dating. I'm not going to lie to you: very occasionally, when I told a man I was a cancer survivor they did cease contact with me. And you know what? That's okay! Because that was the Universe filtering out the wrong men for me. The Universe is my very own personal matchmaker and it keeps me away from those who are not worthy of my fabulousness. It wasn't because I'm 'broken' or 'damaged' or went through cancer treatment that they didn't stick around; it's simply because I wasn't right for them and they weren't right for me.

As soon as I started doing the inner work of accepting myself, falling in love with myself and celebrating who I am inside and out, I started meeting the nicest guys. Guys who respected, admired and liked me more because of what I had been through. It was the Law of Attraction in action. I started truly loving myself, not seeing myself as broken or damaged but as flawed and beautiful. I was putting out the right energy, the right vibes, into the Universe. I was attracting positivity and love into my life simply by feeling positive and loving towards myself.

What matters after cancer treatment isn't the fact you have a non-existent sex drive, that you don't like your partner touching your reconstructed breast or that you worry no one will love you again. What matters is that you focus on loving yourself enough to talk to your partner, to reach out and seek professional help, to pay attention to your issues and your needs. There are ways and there are means to make your love life work, so just be patient with yourself, understand what you are experiencing, speak out and find options that work for you.

Mental health and cancer

There's nothing wrong with you if you feel depressed after cancer treatment.

Maybe I should say that again: there's nothing wrong with you if you feel depressed after cancer treatment.

And there's nothing wrong with reaching out and getting help. In fact, it's without a doubt one of the most loving things you can do for yourself. And let me say this loud and clear for you: admitting you're finding it too hard to cope is not a sign of weakness. In fact, it's the opposite. The most courageous people are the ones who are not afraid to admit their fragility, who speak their truth and find the help they need. Ignoring how bad things are for you is not about being strong; it means you're allowing yourself to be ruled by fear – and that's a weakness.

As long as you don't reach out, you'll feel lonely and disconnected, and the ego will continue to run your life. Isolating ourselves only magnifies the solitude and darkness we feel, and yet, when we struggle, one of the first things we do is hide away. Well, don't. Do something different.

If you're feeling at rock bottom, instead of switching off your phone and creeping under the bed covers, pick up your phone and call someone. I mean *actually call someone* – not text, WhatsApp or anything else.

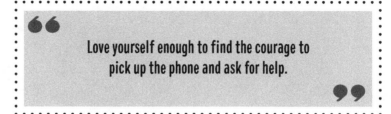

> **Love yourself enough to find the courage to pick up the phone and ask for help.**

In this one, defiant act, you are overcoming the negativity the ego creates in your life. By reaching out and asking for help, you are taking your power back, transforming your life and setting the course for the happiness and peace that rightfully belong to you.

If the depression you're feeling is just too overwhelming, if you're really feeling lost in a black hole, you need to reach out and get professional help. Contact your doctor and ask them to recommend someone you can talk to. Don't suffer in silence; there are mental-health helplines available 24 hours a day, so if you need support, even in the middle of the night, reach out.

So please don't try to tough it out by yourself. Don't ignore the pain or push down the emotions, because that will only make you feel worse. True courage comes with admitting your vulnerability and having the willingness to ask for help. True power comes with admitting that you can't do it all on your own. Loving yourself means not making yourself suffer in silence any more.

CHAPTER 8

Tools to Keep You on the Curly and Wide

Now you've become a whole new version of yourself, why stay on the straight and narrow? Remember, we don't need to be round pegs that fit neatly in round holes any more. We are the cancer misfits, and after what we've been through, we're entitled to live big, brash and beautiful lives of any shape or size we want. Your life ahead is going to be amazing, so why not step out of the box and explore the curly and wide path to happiness and peace, making every day even more gratifying and fulfilling as you go?

Everything in this chapter is here to help make sure you keep strolling happily along that path. As I've said before, you can't just read this book start to finish and expect all your problems to have been solved. The way to transform your life, the way to find the path of happiness and peace and stay on it, is to implement the tools and exercises below every single day. Doing all of these things, some of these things or even just one of these things routinely, each and every day from now on, is the surest way to protect yourself from negativity, anxiety and fear.

I still get bad days occasionally. I wouldn't be human if I didn't. And actually I'm grateful for them because I know it's in those dark moments that my greatest lessons lie; that it's in those difficult times that the greatest change and greatest wisdom occurs. And nowadays, when those bad moments come, I have everything I need to cope with them. So, instead of a bad moment turning into a bad day, bad week, bad month or even a bad year, I use these tools and I soon move on.

So, here are some treasures to keep you on the curly and wide with a big, fat smile on your face.

Random acts of kindness

When I was first diagnosed with cancer, the narcissistic (ego-created) part of myself loved the fact that I now had a justifiable reason to make the whole world revolve around me. But once I learned to turn down the volume of my ego and tune in to my heart, I discovered that making it all about me never made me truly happy. When I step outside my own melodrama, when I remove myself from obsessing about my life, my cancer journey, me, me and more me, and I transfer that attention towards other people, that's when I feel a lasting happiness from deep inside my soul. Eureka!

The quickest way to feel miserable is to dwell on the crap in your life; the quickest way to become depressed is to make everything about you; the quickest way to feel lonely and isolated is to get stuck inside your head with only the annoying ego for company. So how do we stop doing all this? Easy – by distracting ourselves, and one of the best ways to distract yourself from you, you and more you, is by redirecting that focus onto somebody else.

It may sound like I'm contradicting myself here. In earlier parts of the book I've gone on and on about self-love, putting yourself first and making you your number-one priority – and now I'm telling you not to make it all about you after all. But there's a huge difference between self-love and being self-centred. There's a big difference between putting your own wellbeing first, and making the whole world revolve around you.

I am simply stressing the power of human connection. Connecting with others in a loving way is a very powerful tool for overcoming negative feelings and thoughts. When you feel that you're getting sucked back into the ego's whispers about how sh*t your life is, you can ignore it simply by doing something lovely for somebody else. And by doing something lovely for somebody else, you're bringing more loveliness to yourself, thanks to the Law of Attraction I told you about in Chapter 7.

'Your life will become better by making other lives better.'

WILL SMITH

It may sound weird and hard to believe, but random acts of kindness actually benefit the giver as much, if not more, than the beneficiary. By giving to, or doing for, somebody else, you are attracting a lot of positivity back into your life. You're a magnet, remember? So, if you do all kinds of lovely things for others, then all kinds of lovely things will be drawn back to you. Talk about the best things in life being free!

And it gets even better, because the person for whom you do a random act of kindness then pays it forward by being kind to the people they next come into contact with, and so on and so forth. So actually, little old you will have triggered a cascade of kindness and love that affects more people than you could possibly imagine.

One of the ways I implement random acts of kindness in my life is through The Compliment Project, an initiative created by San Francisco-based artist Anna Sergeeva as a way for us all to spread love and positivity. From the project's website (www.thecomplimentproject.org) you download free A4 sheets of different compliments to stick up in random places for strangers to find. And it gets even better: each sheet also has the compliment printed several times on small strips you can tear off and give to a friend. Ingenious! I pretty much always have a stash of these compliment sheets in my bag, along with some sticky tape (I kid you not), and wherever I am – a restaurant, a museum, a department store – I go to the bathroom and stick a couple of them on the mirror at the sinks. It's an easy, quick random act of kindness and it's even better because it's done in secret and nobody knows it was me! I've been out for lunch and returned to the bathroom 30 minutes after putting up one of the sheets to find all the compliment strips had been ripped off and passed along. How cool is that? I also remember putting one up in the bathroom of a hospital's oncology ward, then seeing an exhausted-looking woman, who was clearly going through chemotherapy, approach the sinks. She looked in the mirror and grimaced at her reflection – then she noticed the compliment that I'd stuck to the mirror. Her whole demeanour instantly changed: she smiled at herself and stood that little bit taller. Talk about food for the soul! So, go to the Compliment Project website and try it for yourself. I defy you to feel crap about life after making random strangers feel good about theirs.

Here are some other random acts of kindness to inspire you:

- Let someone go in front of you when you're standing in line at the supermarket or the bank.

- Compliment a stranger – tell them how great they look in that coat, or how their smile is beautiful.

- Buy a coffee for the person standing in line behind you in the coffee shop.

- Surprise a friend with a bunch of flowers for no reason.

- Leave little Post-it notes with positive body-image messages in clothing-store changing rooms, such as 'You are beautiful exactly the way you are right now.'

- Send a text or email to one person every day, thanking them for something, even just: 'Thank you for being you.'

➡ Write a little thank-you note on the bill when you pay your server in a restaurant.

➡ Make everyone feel important; learn the name of the person at your local petrol station or at the corner shop and greet them personally.

➡ Leave a little gift, such as a box of chocolates, for your postman or the rubbish men, just to let them know they're appreciated.

➡ Rather than only ever giving a homeless person money, once in a while buy them some gloves or something hot to eat instead.

➡ Give your seat up on the train or bus, not just to someone who's elderly or pregnant but to someone who looks like they've had a rough day.

➡ If you see a couple trying to take a selfie, offer to take the photo for them.

➡ Send a loved one a handwritten letter – it's become an old-fashioned practice but it's the surest way to make someone's day.

➡ Completely ignore your phone when you're having a conversation – just turn it off.

➡ At a party or event, talk to the shy person who's hiding in the corner.

And don't overthink it. A kindness is a kindness, and even the simplest and easiest gesture can make a huge difference to someone else and to yourself.

Gratitude

Each night, before you go to sleep, write down everything you've been grateful for that day. I don't go to sleep at night until I have written a list of things I've been grateful for that day. It literally takes a minute or two, so there's no excuse not to. Reflect on your day and focus on the things that made you smile – the food that tasted good, the person who was kind, the beauty that you noticed, and so on – then note these down. Your gratitude doesn't have to be for huge, profound things. In fact, writing down the small things we take for granted can be even more powerful, like the feeling of a fresh mouth and clean teeth after brushing. One of my favourites is a simple cold glass of water. Doing this is now as imperative and as important to my daily routine as looking in the mirror and declaring my undying love to myself. And it should be the same for you.

When you go to sleep focused on gratitude, chances are you will wake up feeling positive about the day ahead. I used to go to sleep stressing out, with my brain doing a ballroom dance with the ego inside my head. I'd get into bed and worry about how the side-effects of my medication were probably going to keep me up all night. And guess what? They did. But then I started this whole gratitude thing and, I swear to you, I started sleeping better.

'When gratitude becomes an essential foundation in our lives, miracles start to appear everywhere.'

EMMANUEL DAGHER

Sadly, people tend to underestimate the power of gratitude and the miracles it can bring into our lives. Most of us want quick fixes and instant gratification; we want someone to tell us to do something simple and easy and to be instantly happy with the results. But it's not the end result that matters; it's the beauty of the journey. There's no end destination when it comes to loving yourself and finding true happiness and peace.

So, be grateful every single day, even on the days when you feel like utter crap. Those are the most important days of all to dig deep and find something, anything, to be grateful for. On the crap days, I may just have three things on my gratitude list, like water, my bed and sleep. But I always find something to be grateful for, no matter what.

Here's a great way to focus on all the good stuff in your life right now. Write a list of 50 names of people who have touched your life in some way, whether it be family members, a teacher, a colleague or a famous person you've never met who has inspired you. There's no right or wrong, just as long as you write 50 names. It's impossible not to feel grateful when you see those 50 names and realize how many people have touched your life in some way.

Positivity

It took time for me to become the annoyingly positive person I am today. Awareness of my negativity was the start; catching myself when I was moaning and groaning about my life. And in the beginning I didn't always manage to catch myself in time. I'd start complaining to someone, or wallow in the glorious mud of self-pity, and only a few days later would I realize just how negative I was being. But the point is that I did eventually realize, then I remembered I had the choice to do, think and feel differently. That awareness alone is the first step. So, don't stress if you still experience negative outbursts; it's about progress, not perfection, and as you become more aware, you'll react differently. Keep trying and you'll get the hang of it.

It goes back to that simple and life-changing concept I told you about in Chapter 7: the Law of Attraction – what you put into the world, you'll also receive. Remember the following phrases to help yourself remember to choose positive instead of negative:

➡ What you think, you will create.

➡ What you feel, you will attract.

➡ What you imagine, you will become.

Recite those phrases over and over, and never forget them, because they form the key that can open the door to the greatest chapter of your life. Negative thinking and feeling are only going to attract more negativity. When I made a decision to focus on self-love, on getting to know the new me and on making other people smile and feel loved, guess what happened? Miracles and happiness happened.

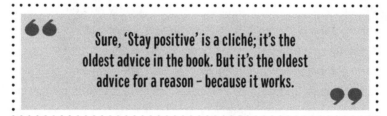

> Sure, 'Stay positive' is a cliché; it's the oldest advice in the book. But it's the oldest advice for a reason – because it works.

But positivity only works if you practise it in some way, every single day. So, let's say you have that dreaded check-up with your oncologist next week and it's all you can think about. The more you think about it, the quicker your fear and anxiety will grow, and inevitably swallow you up in one big fat gulp.

So, don't let it. When you get those negative thoughts in your head, that hollow feeling in your stomach or that panic in your chest, take a deep, long breath and look around you. No, I mean really look around you – not a nonchalant glance around the room. Open your eyes and see the wonder. Perhaps there's a loved one nearby – a relative, friend or pet. Look at them and appreciate how blessed you are to have such a wonderful being in your life. Or look out the window and marvel at the sky, even if it's raining; instead of seeing it as a negative, marvel at the beauty and power of the rain – it quenches the planet's thirst and keeps us all alive. Have a sip of your coffee, tea, juice, wine or whatever. Sip it with delicious intention and attention, focus on the sensations it gives you in your mouth and on your tongue, and appreciate its yumminess. These are just three things to be positive about, but the list is endless. And while you're busy focusing on those things, as your peace and positivity grow, your fear and anxiety – your negativity – will subside. That's how it works. Isn't that marvellous?

So, stop making the wrong choices. Stop giving the negative any life force at all. Start realizing that fear, anxiety and all that crap deserve none of your attention and energy, while the beauty and blessings around you certainly do. Imagine this: you're standing on a footbridge in between two worlds. The world on one side is dark, cold and barren. The trees are bare, there is no life; no wildlife, no people. There is nothing. The world on the other side is like a garden out of a fairy tale. The sun is shining and there's a fragrant fresh breeze in the air. The garden is covered in technicolour flowers and magical wildlife such as hummingbirds and butterflies. You get to choose which side of the bridge you will reside in. You can go either way: it's completely up to you, and whichever one you choose to focus on will become your reality. I know which reality I'd prefer. What about you?

Staying young

Why are we all in such a hurry to grow up? Yes, it's important to be responsible, sensible and practical. But it's also just as important to keep an element of playfulness in our lives.

Most of us are aware of our inner child only when someone points out that we're being childish or immature, as though these qualities represent the worst parts of ourselves. As a consequence, we try to hide or ignore that part of us, instead of recognizing that our inner child actually represents some of the most beautiful traits and characteristics that we have. Your inner child represents your creativity, your excitement and wonder at the world; your delight, curiosity and awe – all those pure and innocent characteristics that haven't been tainted by your life experience.

Staying connected to your inner child means staying connected to the part of yourself that is completely enchanted when it sees a rainbow or gets super-excited about an ice cream on a hot summer's day; the part of you that secretly loves jumping in a puddle, has fun just being goofy and thinks splattering a blob of paint onto a cardboard box is both exciting and beautiful.

The mistake we make is believing we that have to be one or the other: either a responsible adult or an immature kid. But actually, to live your happiest life you need to find a balance between the two. For instance, I'm responsible, I pay my bills on time, I keep my house clean and my life is organized – but at the same I still jump in puddles, get overly excited about ice cream and roll around on the floor with my dogs, laughing so much that I almost pee myself.

You may not have connected to your inner child for a long time, but it's still inside you, just waiting for a little attention. So, next time you're at a restaurant with your kids and the server brings them those paper place mats they can colour in and a mug of crayons, don't just have an adult conversation while they draw and scribble. Ask the server for your own paper place mat, grab a crayon and join in. And if you don't have kids, ask that server for a paper place mat and crayons anyway, and go wild. Trust me: your heart and your soul will love you for it.

When you connect with the childlike part of yourself, you'll realize that the innocent, playful and carefree part of you didn't disappear as you grew up. It's just that you forgot it was there. But if you can remember it and allow your inner child to come out and play from time to time, you'll be amazed at how happy, hopeful and confident you'll start to feel.

Creativity

The best way to connect with your inner child is through creativity. Creativity feeds the soul, and because creativity comes from that innocent, childlike part of ourselves, it is a place where the ego has no involvement, no voice to judge, criticize or condemn. Being creative is also a very healthy way to express and release any bottled-up negativity keeping you in darkness.

The good news is that anyone and everyone can be creative. You don't have to be Van Gogh to pick up a paintbrush; you don't have to be J.K. Rowling to write a story and you don't have to be Jamie Oliver to come up with your own recipes.

> 'Every child is an artist. The problem is how to remain an artist when they grow up.'
> **PABLO PICASSO**

Creativity can be all kinds of things. Creativity is when you go for a walk on the beach and write 'I Love Life' or 'Hope Conquers All' in giant letters in the sand. Creativity can be as simple as learning something new, like playing the trumpet or dancing salsa. If you struggle with being creative, I recommend you read the brilliant book *The Artist's Way* by Julia Cameron, which was a huge stepping stone on my journey to happiness and taught me to find that place where my creativity flows most freely.

Here are some ideas for how to reconnect with your inner child and get creative:

Reconnect with past passions

What activities did you love to do as a kid? Roller-skating, horse riding, go-kart racing? Just because you're an adult, it doesn't mean you have to stop enjoying them.

Colouring in for adults

There's a plethora of adults' colouring books available nowadays; it's become cool to go back to doing this, just like when you were a kid, and it's a great method for mindfulness and releasing stress. I promise you that zoning out by making sure you colour within the lines is the quickest way to take your mind off negative fear-based thoughts.

Scrapbooking

This may sound like something your grandma would do, but I do it all the time and I'm the coolest cat I know. Scrapbooking can be a healthy and creative way to express what's going on for you right now, whether that be negative thoughts and feelings or positive ones. I find scrapbooking a creative way to release emotions that have been building up inside me. So, for example, if I'm having a sad day, instead of avoiding my feelings and just hiding under the covers, I'll put on some lovely, soothing music and try to express how I'm feeling through the images and words I cut out from magazines and stick into my scrapbook along with some poems, quotes or scribbled doodles. There's no right or wrong with scrapbooking. You can write, stick or doodle whatever you want, and that's why I dig it so much – it's creative freedom, which makes my inner child very happy indeed.

Tap into your inner author

Grab your laptop, journal or a paper napkin, and start writing. Don't think, just write whatever comes to you; tap into your heart and allow whatever it is that wants to be expressed to flow through your pen onto the paper – or through your fingers onto the keyboard.

Redecorate a room

Paint the walls a different colour (preferably not beige) and bring some brightness into your home. I painted my sitting room a cool dirty-pink colour simply because the name of the paint was Unicorn Horn. I wanted my sitting room to be painted the colour of a unicorn horn because, quite frankly, it doesn't get cooler than that. If you're not into repainting, then go and get some crazy curtains or a cool poster, or rearrange all the pictures on your wall that have been hanging in the same place for way too long. You could print out your favourite positive quotes or affirmations, get them framed and add those to your collection.

Get cooking

Get in the kitchen and start creating your own recipes. If that's a bit too big and scary, follow someone else's recipe but make sure you add one new ingredient so that you're getting creative and making the dish uniquely yours.

Share yourself

Create your own blog or podcast and spread a little happiness in cyberspace.

Learn something new

Exploring something new that you've never tried is a way of letting your inner child come out to play. So, take classes in something you've always been fascinated by or wanted to do, like star-gazing, upholstery or speaking Chinese.

Do something random

Fly a kite, build a sandcastle, learn how to juggle or join a rock 'n' roll band.

Go toy shopping

Explore your local toyshop and buy one thing for your inner child – maybe a temporary-tattoo kit, or sequin-sticking kit to cover your things in sparkliness. No grown-up purchases allowed.

Go to the movies

But you're only allowed to see a kid's movie – one that makes you forget normality and the seriousness of day-to-day life. Animated films are great for this as they're full of colour, goofiness and positivity. It's also mandatory to buy a fizzy drink and some sweets – sure, they're bad for you, but it's loving to spoil your inner child once in a while.

Play the games you used to love

Gather some friends or family and play the games you used to love as a kid. Charades is a great way to get the creative juices flowing; Twister uses creative thinking to come with up new ways to contort your body into weird and wonderful shapes and poses. And playing games like these won't just bring out your own inner child – everyone else's inner child will come out to play too.

All the suggestions above will allow your inner child to come out and get creative. For even more ideas, try searching online for creative activities for kids. You'll find so much inspiration, you won't know what to do first.

Meditation

When I started meditation, I hated it. I'm impatient at the best of times, so asking me to sit and stay completely still was a very tall order. But that doesn't mean I didn't try it, and it doesn't mean I gave up after a week because I couldn't do it perfectly.

My happiness and peace were top-priority to me, so I just kept trying. I might not have been doing the greatest job, but I did it for 10 minutes every day anyway. That was years ago and now, some days, I meditate for up to an hour because the peace, positivity and transformation it brings me are invaluable. And just as importantly, I now actually love doing it. Who knew? So, don't give up before you've given it a proper chance.

Meditation isn't just for experts of yoga, monks or enlightened beings; meditation is for people like me and it's for people like you.

For me, meditation is like spirituality in that you get to create your own version, to suit whatever works and feels comfortable for you. I think that's part of the reason so many people squirm at the thought of starting meditation: they assume there's only one way to do it, which involves sitting in total silence for 30 minutes and completely clearing their head of any thoughts. And yes, that's what meditation is for some people, but it's most certainly not like this for everyone. I have my own methods and techniques of meditation that work for me – some involve sitting in silence and clearing my thoughts, and some don't. Sometimes I meditate in order to still my thoughts so I can connect with the Universe and my Higher Power. Sometimes I meditate to sit and be in the negative feelings that are coming up for me, because my meditation gives me a safe space to feel the pain and to heal it. And sometimes I use Law of Attraction-based meditations I've found on the internet, to help me manifest the future I dream about and long for.

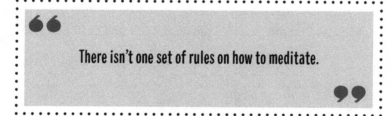

There isn't one set of rules on how to meditate.

If you've never meditated before, here is the best way to describe it. Imagine you're curled up on the sofa watching television. You're not watching anything particularly intellectual or stimulating – just a cheesy comedy series or reality show. You get to that point where you just feel completely chilled out and, as this term so perfectly puts it, you veg out, sitting there like a cabbage, or like a warm, soft baked potato. If you now took the remote control and switched off the television, but stayed exactly where you were in that chilled, vegetative state, and closed your eyes... that's pretty much what meditation feels like. When I meditate, it feels as though I'm a teaspoon of sugar dissolving into a warm cup of tea, only the tea is the Universe and I am dissolving into everything.

There are so many psychological benefits to meditation, such as being able to self-heal and self-soothe, to be present and to acknowledge the feelings you're experiencing; to no longer be a suffering victim powerless in the face of negative emotion. I'm not saying meditation is an overnight cure to all your woes, but ask anyone who has incorporated meditation into their daily life if they feel any difference, and I'm 100 per cent certain that the consensus would be a big, fat, chilled-out and happy-as-can-be YES.

If you find that you're constantly distracted while trying to meditate, or deafened by the noise in your mind, it doesn't mean you suck at meditation. It means you're facing the same challenges as every single other person who meditates. What's important is having the discipline and motivation to go through that noise in order to reach the other side. Meditation is like an ocean: sometimes it's calm and easy to float, but sometimes it's stormy, the waves are choppy, and you're tossed all over the place. Someone once described it to me like this: the more your thoughts distract you while in meditation, the more opportunities you have to reconnect to yourself and the powers beyond.

So, love and accept yourself, even if you seem to suck at meditating, because if you keep trying, one day you won't suck at it any more.

Research into the benefits of meditation* shows that it:

➡ Reduces stress, and therefore the hazards of illnesses where stress is a factor – like cancer

➡ Relieves depression, anxiety and fear

➡ Improves empathy, with a positive impact on relationships

➡ Lengthens attention span and promotes better memory function

➡ Enhances pain management

➡ Inspires creativity

➡ Slows down the ageing process, rejuvenates and revitalizes

➡ Promotes better sleep

➡ Decreases feelings of loneliness

➡ Aids emotional and spiritual self-healing

I could go on and on, but this list should already have convinced you that meditation is pretty powerful stuff. So, if you haven't started meditating yet, it's time to download a meditation app like Insight Timer (my favourite) and get started.

Positive affirmations

Here are three positive affirmations about positive affirmations:

---

* Thorpe, M. (2017), '12 Science-Based Benefits of Meditation', *Healthline*, https://www.healthline.com/nutrition/12-benefits-of-meditation [accessed 4 August 2020]

➡ Positive affirmations influence your subconscious to trigger positive transformation.

➡ Positive affirmations refigure, retune and recreate your thoughts and your feelings.

➡ Positive affirmations transform negative thinking and painful emotions.

To affirm something is simply to declare that it's true, and the more positive things you affirm, the more you make positive things, thoughts, feelings, dreams and desires become the truth and, ultimately, your reality.

I kid you not: affirmations can be that powerful.

I used to be constantly preoccupied with the future, with the notion of 'One day...': *One day, when I don't feel like a cancer victim any more...*; *One day, when I've lost more weight...*; *One day, when my hair's longer...*; *One day, blah blah blah...* I used to be so busy thinking about how happy and awesome my life would be 'one day' that I completely ignored the fact that I can choose to see and create the awesome in my life *today*. But ever since I started incorporating daily positive affirmations into my life, I've started to be more present and to notice the positive and good in the here and now, which means I create even more of it.

Positive affirmations made me realize that I always have a choice; I can choose to dwell on the negative or reprogram myself to focus on the positive. I can choose to hold on to the pain or to let the pain go; to crawl into the darkness or walk into the light.

> 'Affirmations are our mental vitamins, providing the supplementary positive thoughts we need to balance the barrage of negative events and thoughts we experience daily.'
>
> TIA WALKER, *THE INSPIRED CAREGIVER*

I've finally understood that yes, bad things do happen, but it's not the bad things or 'bad luck' that block our path with so many of these titanium hurdles, it's our negative thoughts about them – our own stinking thinking. It's our own thoughts that create these humongous blocks that keep us stuck in the fear. When I believed there was no way I could be truly happy after the hell of cancer treatment, my life wasn't happy. At the time, I couldn't understand why I was so unbelievably depressed and had no hope for the future, but in hindsight I completely understand why I was stuck there – it was because I constantly told myself negative things like:

I'll never be as pretty as I used to be.

I'll never feel confident again.

I am damaged and broken now.

Of course I was going to stay stuck, if that was what I was telling myself. Which is why I decided to do something different, to try to change the record that was replaying the same crap over and over in my head. But I couldn't just click my fingers and change the way I was thinking. I had to retrain my brain, my mind, my thoughts and my feelings. And I did this by plastering positive affirmations all over my house and saying them out loud to myself every day.

I have affirmed to myself that 'I am beautiful just the way I am, right here, right now' so many times that I now 100 per cent believe it.

I have told myself so many times that 'I am more than enough and can do anything I set my mind to' that I got a book deal with my dream publishers, and you're reading it right now.

And I have repeated to myself so often that 'I deserve the best and accept the best now' that miracles just keep happening to me.

By repeating positive affirmations day in and day out, I retrained my mind and heart to believe them. It's inevitable: if, every day, you tell yourself something positive that goes against a pessimistic thought or feeling that you've had your whole life, you will eventually reprogram yourself and completely change your point of view, and as a consequence change your life.

As I mentioned in Chapter 5, when I first started with affirmation work I had no clue what I was doing, so I found affirmations from other people who did, such as Louise Hay. But as time passed and affirmations became second nature to me, I felt the need to make my daily affirmations more personal and more concurrent to the things going on in my life. For example, if there was a week when I was waiting to receive some cancer-related test results, I'd write my own affirmation for that specific reason, such as: 'I choose to have complete faith that my body is whole, happy and healthy right now.'

So, below is a selection of affirmations to make specific to you, your life and what you currently want to focus on. If this seems a bit too much for you right now, just stick to the examples in Chapter 5, and when you feel more confident, you can start making up your own.

⇨ PERSONALIZE YOUR AFFIRMATIONS ⇦

As with the exercise in Chapter 5, write down each affirmation on its own Post-it note (choose whichever ones resonate with you), fill in the blank then put it up somewhere in your home where you're going to see it every day, such as on the fridge, in the car, opposite where you sit on the toilet, in your wallet and on the front door so you'll see it whenever you leave the house. Whenever you see one, say it out loud – and when you say the words, say them not from your head, but from your heart.

➡ I deserve to be _____ (happy, at peace, surrounded by love, etc.) and I am now _____ (happy, at peace, surrounded by love etc.).

➡ Every day, in every possible, wonderful way, I am getting _____ (healthier, happier, more confident, etc.).

➡ I am completely worthy of being _____ (successful, ridiculously happy, hopelessly in love, etc.).

➡ I'm allowed to have _____ (freedom, peace, joy, etc.) and I do.

⮕ I love myself just the way I am today because I am _____ (more than enough, fantastic, beautiful, capable of great things, etc.).

⮕ I am so happy and grateful that I have so much _____ (love, peace, contentment, success, etc.) in my life.

⮕ I will not allow _____ (fear, other people, cancer, etc.) to take away my joy. I deserve to be happy now.

⮕ I dream of being _____ (confident, full of life, successful, at peace etc.). My dream is coming true right now.

⮕ I choose _____ (inner peace, self-belief, total happiness, etc.) and it flows into my life now.

⮕ I am so happy and grateful now that I am _____ (receiving so much abundance, enjoying so much love in my life, feeling so sexy and beautiful, etc.)

You can also incorporate your daily affirmations into your meditation practice, too. Simply choose a particular affirmation and repeat it in your mind over and over again as a mantra while you meditate.

Prayer

I know I already suggested prayer to you in Chapter 4, but it's such a ninja-like spiritual tool to completely transform your life that I'm going to stress its importance to you again. I'm aware that for those of us who aren't religious, the word 'prayer' can be a little bit icky and uncomfortable. We assume that if we don't believe in God or follow a particular faith path, then prayer is not an option for us. But prayer doesn't necessarily mean getting down on your knees and reciting 'Our Father'.

In this day and age, with all things mind, body and spirit becoming more and more mainstream, prayer is no longer synonymous just with religion. The act of prayer is simply our individual and very personal way to communicate with our Higher Power of choice, whether that be God, the Universe, Mother Earth, Life Energy or anything else. It's simply a vertical conversation with the powers that be, rather than a horizontal conversation with other people.

There is no wrong or right way to pray. It doesn't matter how you choose to converse with your Higher Power, just as long as you keep the conversation going so you can stay connected to its powerful positive energy. Keeping that connection strong also means the ego has less of a chance to be a bad influence in your life and to bring you down.

'Our prayers may be awkward. Our attempts may be feeble. But since the power of prayer is in the one who hears it and not in the one who says it, our prayers do make a difference.'

MAX LUCADO, *HE STILL MOVES STONES*

Regular conversation, or prayer, with your Higher Power enables you to remain open and available to its guidance and wisdom, and you'll begin to realize that you have all the support you could possibly need. Through prayer, you can ask questions and receive answers, share your predicaments and find solutions, and hand over feelings you don't like and don't want to deal with, such as anger, fear, resentment and shame.

Prayer can ease depression and act as a cushion when life throws you all over the place. The next time you've had a bad day, before you pour another glass of wine, call Deliveroo to order an extra-large pizza, or just pull the covers over your head and sleep to avoid the feelings, remember to have a chat with your Higher Power first. Actually remembering to do this is really important. It's a bit like wanting to win the lottery but not buying a ticket. Your Higher Power – whether it's God, the Universe or Yoda – can't help you unless you remember to reach out and actually ask it to.

Acceptance

I believe the key to a happy, peaceful and confident life is acceptance – accepting yourself exactly the way you are, and no longer comparing yourself to how you used to be. It's about accepting life's circumstances and present situations – just going with the flow instead of fighting the current, because while you continue to fight against it you'll be living in a place of struggle and frustration. It's about accepting all that is, and choosing to see the positive, to see beauty and abundance, instead of focusing only on the negative, on pain and lack.

For some reason, we all have an innate yearning to be perfect – to look perfect, to feel perfect, to work perfectly, love perfectly and to recover from cancer treatment perfectly.

But there's no such thing as perfect, and as far as I'm concerned that word should be removed from the dictionary altogether. Perfection is completely unobtainable and the only thing it does is make sure we never feel good enough, that our lives never seem happy enough, peaceful enough, successful enough or pretty enough. But enough of not feeling enough!

The Cambridge Dictionary definition of perfection is 'the state of being complete and correct in every way' while the Merriam-Webster dictionary describes it as 'freedom from fault or defect'. Talk about pressure. We need to learn to love ourselves and our lives as they are: flawed, scarred and beautifully imperfect. It's those parts of ourselves that makes us our most beautiful, and those parts of our lives that offer the greatest growth and positive transformation.

Accept yourself, accept your life, accept how you're feeling right now in this moment and stop placing so many unrealistic demands on yourself and having such high expectations for your recovery from treatment.

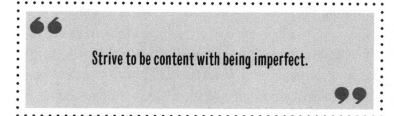

Strive to be content with being imperfect.

Before you finish this book, make a commitment to yourself that you will, from now on, be more accepting of yourself, of others and of life in general. That instead of asking, *Why me? Why did this happen? Why does it have to be like this? Why can't it be more like that?* You will try to say, *I may not understand, but I choose to trust and to go with the flow of the Universe and the flow of my life.* This simple commitment to yourself could be all it takes to break open the dam and let all of the good things you're longing for flow freely to you.

Acceptance is about letting go of controlling everything, of insisting you know what's best for yourself, because most of the time you don't. Most of the time, the way you think and feel – the things you want to do, what you believe to be right – are not actually in your best interest. Instead, hand over the steering wheel of your life to your Higher Power and start trusting and accepting the process, instead of trying to steer your life in the direction you think you want to go. Shimmy over to the passenger seat, put on your seat belt, wind down the window, feel the breeze on your face and just enjoy the ride. Let your Higher Power do the driving. Your Higher Power wants you to live your greatest life and it knows the way you should be going in order to get there.

The journey may not always be plain sailing – you may get motion sickness, you may break down a few times, there may be storms that blow over trees that then block the way. But remember, it's all integral and vital to the experience of your beautiful life.

> **All the twists and turns serve a purpose, even if you don't know what that purpose is.**

You just need to trust that none of it's in vain and that life lessons are being learned that will transform you for the better.

I know what I'm asking is not easy: to simply trust, accept and let go; to have blind faith and believe that your Higher Power has reasons for everything, even the bad stuff that happens in your life. I know that's a big ask, and yes, I understand you have plenty of reasons why this doesn't resonate with you. But I'm telling you this because life is a lot more easy, flowing and joyous if you can just make peace with what is. I'm not justifying the fact you got cancer. I'm not saying it's fair, right or okay. I'm saying, it is what it is, and you can either stomp your feet and scream at the unfairness or accept that this is your journey and choose to focus on the beauty in your life, no matter what.

Acceptance is the ultimate gift you can bestow upon yourself; to try to see anything and everything that happens in your life through eyes of positivity instead of the pessimistic and defeatist eyes of the ego. I'm not saying that when something bad happens, like when a loved one dies or you lose your job, you must instantly find the positives in the pain of that situation. Of course, I'm not saying that. Feel the pain, feel whatever it is you're feeling, just don't get stuck in the darkness and negativity and let it take over your whole life. Be willing to see even a glimpse of good in the bad.

When I recently lost a loved one, it was emotional agony. Grief is the most painful of all emotions, and I felt as though I might die from it. But at the same time as grieving my loss, I tried to focus on the idea that wherever that person is now, wherever their beautiful soul has gone, in that place there is no struggle, no hardship, no cancer and no more of the uphill climbs we have to contend with here on Earth. I felt the pain, but I also chose to imagine the person's soul as happy, at peace and free.

If I do lose my job, no doubt I'll panic, feel overwhelmed by financial fear and be anxious about the future. But I'll also choose to believe that the Universe didn't want that job for me because it has something even better in store. I'll feel the pain, but I'll still choose to hold on to trust and hope, no matter what.

Your life is always going to be unpredictable, no matter how hard you try to control it. Everything is constantly changing, and all I'm asking is that you just try to go with the flow of life, to try your very best to accept those changes and embrace them the best way you can.

Imagination

Dare to dream big.

Dare to dream bigger than big.

Dare to dream huge, gigantic, colossal, enormous, gargantuan dreams.

I never dared to dream big and so (surprise, surprise) amazing things never used to happen for me.

But how can incredibleness ever happen if you don't dare to put it out there? If you don't dare to dream, the Universe gets the impression you don't think it's possible, and if you don't think it's possible yourself, then the Universe won't think it's possible, either.

When I was growing up, the people closest to me told me it's better to be realistic and not dream big, because if you dream big you'll only be disappointed. But they couldn't have got it more wrong if they'd tried. It's the other way around: if you don't dare to dream, then you'll always be disappointed. But if you dream big enough and loud enough for the Universe to hear, then you'd better stand back and get ready to watch the magic happen.

I always wanted to be an author, but I never believed I could. When I was around 11 or 12 years old, I was told I had as much chance of getting a book published as I did of winning the lottery. And all my life I believed that, so I didn't bother to try or even dream I could do it. But thankfully, due to the transformation I went through after cancer treatment, I stopped believing this; I stopped believing the negative and 'realistic' voices around me, and I stopped believing my ego too. I dared to dream I could do it, and I did it.

'Imagination is everything. It is the preview of life's coming attractions.'

ALBERT EINSTEIN

I know I've asked you to meditate daily, which is already a big inconvenience because it's swallowing a whole 10 minutes of your day, but I have another favour to ask you. I want you to give up another five minutes each day to make your dreams come true. You can do this when you're having a bath, when you're walking the dog, on the way back from work or from dropping the kids at school, or just before you go to sleep. This is about making your dreams come true, so do what you can to find that five-minute slot in your day, and read on.

For five minutes every day, I want you to imagine your ideal life and that you're living it right now. The more detailed the picture in your imagination, the more opportunity you're giving the Universe to manifest exactly what you want.

Dream about each beautiful little detail, like feeling super-healthy in your body, smelling the fragrant flowers in the garden of your dream home, or waking up and knowing you get to do what you love and to be surrounded by incredible people. If you want to live in a beach house in Hawaii, imagine that you already live there. If you want to be a bestselling author, imagine yourself at a book signing with a line of people around the block waiting for you to sign their copy of your latest *New York Times* bestseller. If you dream of running a marathon, imagine what it feels like to cross the finish line, then the taste of what you'll be eating as your celebratory meal.

The way to make your dreams come true is to believe with 100 per cent conviction that they will happen; that it isn't matter of 'if', just a matter of 'when'.

You can take that exercise one step further with a vision board. A vision board is effectively a montage of images representing the life of your dreams. You can do it the old-skool way, using clippings from magazines, or with internet searches and a photo-editing app. And you can update your board every few months if you feel your vision has changed. Mine is more of a vision wall, actually; a wall covered in my dreams. And as if that weren't enough, I keep a copy of these images – my dreams – in a small envelope in my bag. The envelope simply has 'My Dreams' written on the front, and it goes with me everywhere. If I'm sitting on a busy rush-hour train or I'm bored senseless waiting for a doctor's appointment, I look through the pictures and allow my imagination to take me away from that packed, sweaty train carriage or dour hospital waiting room and into my beautiful, wood-cabin-style house nestled in a forest somewhere. (Yup, I'm moving to the forest one day. Just you wait and see.)

Wanna know how big I'm dreaming? I downloaded a photo of Oprah Winfrey interviewing someone in her garden in Hawaii and, using a photo-editing app, I replaced the interviewee's head with mine. Now I have a photo on my vision wall of Oprah interviewing me! I've made it look as if it's already happened. I even imagine how nervous I am before the interview, and how afterwards we natter in her kitchen about how much we adore our dogs. I dream it in enormous detail because I intend to make it real. I hope you're hearing me, Universe!

And here's proof that visioning works. A few years ago, I found a photo on the internet showing all the Hay House authors on a stage together, arms in the air, celebrating. Then I chose a photo of myself and, on my computer, pasted it in front of them all so it looked like they were celebrating me. I blew it up to A4 size and put it on my vision wall. Check out who the publisher of this book is: Hay House, baby!

My dream of becoming a Hay House author came true, and I believe I manifested that dream into reality because I refused to believe it wouldn't happen. It wasn't about 'if' I was going to be a Hay House author; it was only about 'when' I'd be joining the Hay House tribe. I believed it so much that the Universe 100 per cent agreed and made my dream come true. I am the proof that dreams come true.

So, what have you got to lose by dreaming, and by printing out a few photos of your wishes and desires? Nothing. But what will you gain if you start dreaming as big as I do? Everything and more. All you've got to do is believe it's possible and the Universe will prove to you that it is.

> 'What if dreaming the impossible dream enough times begins to make the impossible possible?'
>
> **DEBBIE DIXON, *THE PATH TO FREEDOM***

CHAPTER 9

Ready, Steady, Go!

This is the last chapter of the book, which means it's time for you to get ready to go out into this big, beautiful world and start living the greatest chapter of your life so far. You've got all the tools, wisdom and inspiration you need to live confidently, happily and at peace. There's no time-estimate for when you should be ready to truly move on with your life after cancer treatment, so just trust the process and take baby steps instead of giant leaps.

Don't be overwhelmed by the idea of implementing all of the practices in this book into your life every day. It is achievable, but only if you take it one small step at a time. No Olympic long jumps please; think small but purposeful strides, like an infant learning to walk. This is a new way of being for you, a new way of living. So, think of yourself as that small child taking its first cautious but deliberate steps.

'Baby step - a tentative act or measure which is the first stage in a long or challenging process.'

OXFORD ENGLISH DICTIONARY

We all seem to be in such a hurry all the time. Even when we have no particular place to be, we rush down the street as though we're already late. It has become normal to rush, to get to the end destination as soon as humanly possible. We've become so fixated on the end game, the desired result, that we fail to enjoy all the glorious progress we're making along the way.

Each baby step you take on your journey after treatment – each time you say an affirmation out loud, find ten minutes to meditate, write a gratitude list or do something truly kind and loving for yourself – is a moment when you're experiencing the happiness, confidence and peace you so long for. You're not doing these things to *get to* a place, you're doing them because by doing them you're *in* that place. And the more you do them, the happier, more peaceful and more confident you'll become.

Each small step you take is a big victory. If you go out there and ask the happiest and most successful people how they got to where they are, chances are they'll tell you that they didn't get there overnight. They'll probably tell you they took baby steps in the right direction each and every day; they made one positive choice after another, and as a consequence their life transformed for the better. That's what's most important here:

that you keep going forward, that in those moments when you want to curl up into a ball and disappear, you choose differently – you take something you learned from this book and do that instead. Even if it's just picking up the phone and calling a friend – it may not seem like a big deal but it's an essential step in the right direction. So, celebrate each baby step you take, and be proud of yourself for trying.

At the beginning of my journey it all felt like a complete waste of time. It seemed that I was making all this effort to implement all these new behaviours, but I was still feeling like crap. Then things just started to shift. I started having small moments of hope – snippets of feeling truly happy, seconds of accepting myself and actually starting to see the positives in my life. All the tiny little steps I had already taken began to add up and the magic started to happen. And because I've never stopped implementing those changes – even to this day, more than six years since I started my journey on a spiritual path, I still use all the tools and exercises in this book – I just get happier and happier.

We all fall down

You're not going to get it right all of the time. You might not even get it right most of the time. And that's perfectly okay.

I'm not gonna bullsh*t you and say I get it right all the time either: that I meditate perfectly, without ever letting a thought pop into my head; that I never get hoodwinked by the ego's manipulative whisperings; or that I have a smile of love and gratitude on my face all of the time.

Whatever. I'm human just like you. I trip up and I fall down. The difference is that I used to fall down and stay down, because the ego would take that bad moment and use it to keep me flat on my face for as long as possible. But the new me has the tools I need to get back up, wipe myself down and keep on going.

Self-love is about slipping up, having the bad days and loving ourselves despite them, forgiving ourselves and, most importantly, having compassion for ourselves and how we're feeling. So, give yourself permission to fall down, but don't give yourself permission to stay there. On the difficult days, don't beat yourself up about the fact that you're struggling, because if you're hard on yourself you'll just stay stuck. If you berate yourself for not getting it right, for taking one step back instead of forward, then you're letting the ego win.

'Everyone falls down. Getting back up is how you learn how to walk.'

WALT DISNEY

This isn't a perfect journey. Life itself isn't a perfect journey. We're all here just doing the best we can with what we have. Each day that we try, each day that we're willing to love and accept ourselves and our circumstances exactly the way they are, is a day of beauty and progress. It's the same even on those days when we fall to our knees, because it's in those moments of darkness that we have the choice to get back up. And every time we get back up, we get to reconnect with our heart, our soul and our Higher Power all over again, and that's a beautiful and powerful thing. Falling down is temporary. Only giving up is permanent.

My father used to say to me, 'All you can do is your best,' and I'm saying the same thing to you now. As long as you're trying, as long as you are doing the best you can, that will always be good enough. You're human, and part of being human is getting it wrong, because each time we fall down, each time we get it wrong, we learn a lesson, we know a little more, so next time we can handle it better.

We all fall down – even Buddha, Jesus and Mother Teresa fell down. Falling down is part of the process: it's how we learn and it's how we get more resilient and continue to become the greatest version of ourselves.

Maintenance and upkeep

We all have the best intentions when reading a self-help book or attending a workshop or retreat. We promise ourselves that we'll continue to practise what we've learned every day for the rest of our lives, but two weeks later we're no longer doing it. But if you truly want to move on after cancer treatment and don't want to be haunted by the fear, anxiety and ego, you must incorporate some of what I've given you into your day-to-day existence, permanently.

> Quite simply, I'm as happy as I am today
> because I still use so many of the suggestions
> and exercises that I've given you.

They've become as routine to me as brushing my teeth. Sure, it means I give up an extra half an hour in bed to do my spiritual practice every morning, but then my day flows, I focus on the positives and great things happen, so it's worth it. If I miss my spiritual practice in the morning, I'm anxious before I even walk out the front door, the day's circumstances get overwhelming and everything seems to go wrong. So, it's non-negotiable, because I'll do whatever I have to in order to be happy.

If you use the gifts I've offered you, your life will transform. And when your life does start changing for the better, when one day you realize that you're now living the greatest chapter of your life so far, don't use that as an excuse to stop implementing the tools and exercises that got you there. After all, you don't go to the gym, work your ass off to lose weight and get a great body only to stop going to the gym when you reach your target weight and look fabulous. No, you keep going to the gym to maintain your achievement, to make sure you keep looking and feeling as hot as you do. And it's the same thing when maintaining yourself emotionally, mentally and spiritually. So, keep using the techniques I've shared with you, like the mirror work and meditation, as part of your everyday life and not only will you transform your life to one of peace and happiness, it'll stay like that for good.

⇨ THE CANCER MISFIT'S TO-DO LIST ⇦

Life after cancer treatment can be impossibly hard, but by remembering all of the nuggets of gold in the list below, life after treatment can very possibly become joyous and easy. In a beautiful, happy, confident and peaceful nutshell, here are the things you need to remember:

➡ Allow all feelings – there are no bad or wrong ways to feel.

➡ Stay connected to your heart, your spiritual self and your Higher Power.

➡ Own your strengths and be loving towards your weaknesses.

➡ Accept and love yourself when you trip up and fall down. This is normal and you can easily get back up.

➡ Always practise self-forgiveness, self-compassion and self-love.

➡ Dance.

➡ Meditate, even if it's just for 10 minutes each day.

➡ Practise random acts of kindness (anonymous ones are the best kind).

➡ Put yourself in good company, with those who uplift and don't wallow in negativity

➡ Reach out when you need help.

➡ Set healthy boundaries.

➡ Be creative every day.

➡ Always question where your thoughts and feelings are coming from – your head or your heart?

➡ Don't believe what the ego tells you, and use the tools you have to quieten the ego down.

Look up at the sky more often, smile and say thank you for everything you have to be grateful for.

Just do it

I had stage-three cancer. I don't know if, or when, it will come back, but even if it does come back, I still intend to be happy. I still intend to use the tools I've told you about in this book because they'll stop fear from taking over my life; because no matter how sh*t things get, I'll still be able to dwell on the light and not get sucked back into the darkness.

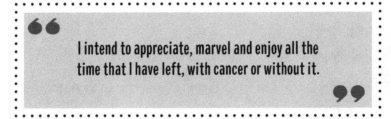

> **I intend to appreciate, marvel and enjoy all the time that I have left, with cancer or without it.**

Take random acts of kindness, for example. Each time I do one it feels like I'm taking a sort of non-pharmaceutical happy pill, even if I've only sent someone a smiley emoji with a few words like 'Hope you're having a beautiful day.' On your tough days, a tiny random act of kindness like that is all you need to do. It might seem small and insignificant – you might think, how can texting such a brief message to someone possibly impact your wellbeing and give you an instant happy buzz? But it does – it really, really does. The more love and happiness you send out, the more love and happiness the Universe will send back to you.

Meditating for ten minutes every day will completely change your life. There's just no way it can't. But it takes a while to get used to it, and if you give up before the magic has had a chance to start, then you'll never know. Even if your thoughts spin around your head like a fairground ride while you meditate, don't give up. Every time a thought distracts you, it's just a perfect excuse to reconnect to your heart; it's part of the meditation process. So just keep trying.

Saying in the mirror every day that you love yourself is going to feel weird for a while. It felt embarrassing, fake and way too uncomfortable for me for a long time. *But I kept doing it anyway.* And I swear this exercise alone has had an incredibly powerful and profound effect on how I feel about myself. It was all I needed to truly start to understand the meaning of self-love; to really start falling in love with myself exactly the way I am after cancer treatment. It took time but it was worth it. So, don't give up on this exercise before you get to experience the miracle.

Happiness, confidence and peace after cancer treatment will come from your persistence, and with each and every baby step you take. So, make sure you take a teeny, tiny step of some sort every day. It's about having the willingness to change and the enthusiasm to try, and trusting that your Higher Power is with you on this journey.

After a little time has passed, you'll look back and realize that somehow, without even knowing you were doing it, you've climbed over a mountain and made it to the other side.

The Unbroken

There is a brokenness
out of which comes the unbroken,
a shatteredness
out of which blooms the unshatterable.

There is a sorrow
beyond all grief which leads to joy
and a fragility
out of whose depths emerges
strength.

There is a hollow space
too vast for words
through which we pass with each loss,
out of whose darkness
we are sanctioned into being.

There is a cry deeper than all sound
whose serrated edges cut the heart
as we break open to the place inside
which is unbreakable and whole,
while learning to sing.

RASHANI RÉA

Acknowledgements

I would like to thank:

Angela Sawano (my mum) – for being my whole family in one person and my greatest teacher.

Takashi Sawano – for always being so good to mum and such a great ally to me.

Barnaby – for being the E.T. to my Elliott.

Bam Bam – for almost 14 years of unconditional canine love and shnuggling me after every chemo treatment. I will miss you every day.

Alex Newby and the team at Hay House – for brilliant editing skills and making my dream a reality.

Lara – for believing in me when I didn't believe in myself.

Gabby Lichtenstern – for being my niece and my friend, and keeping me connected to the younger generation.

Sarah Parker – for being my kindred soul and companion to trippy new realms.

Johan Hultman – for making me laugh so much I nearly pee myself.

David Labua – for his friendship, kindness and wisdom.

Irene Boeddinghaus – for being such an incredible oncologist.

Serena and Mairi at The Hoffman Process – for giving me the first step out of a very dark hole.

Lety and Andy – for being the best doggy uncle and aunt in the world.

Liz Saunders – for never letting me give up on myself and always popping cards in the post.

Hollie and Robert Holden – for everything you are and everything you do.

Tara Halliday – for introducing me to the concept of unconditional love.

Emilee Garfield – for her contagious joy and beautiful heart.

Sammy Horscroft – for always making my hair look great and for the spiritual chit-chat.

Daniella Santangeli – for being my kindred spiritual nut job right around the corner.

Fran Hales – for her friendship and brilliant photos.

Draupadi – for being my fairy godmother.

Abby – for being my fairy ballerina little sister.

Devi Kaur – for making me fall in love with Kundalini.

Louise Hay – for teaching me how to love myself.

Ram Dass – for setting the example of how a human should be.

All my Instagram followers for always supporting me, especially @manycallme_tim, @justice.n.khokar, @glhunter9, @fauxhawk07 and @itsjustahiccup.

All my amazing fellow cancer survivors who contributed to this project.

And last but not least: God, Goddess, Mother Nature, Universe, Gaia, Pachamama, ACIM, my angels, spirit guides of my highest good, ancestors and loved ones who have passed over.

Resources

Transforming your life

Dispenza, J. (2012), *Breaking the Habit of Being Yourself: How to Lose Your Mind and Create a New One*. London: Hay House UK.

Hicks, E. and Hicks, J. (2006), *The Law of Attraction: The Basics of the Teachings of Abraham*. New York: Hay House.

The Compliment Project **www.thecomplimentproject.org**

The Hoffman Process **www.hoffmaninstitute.co.uk**

The spiritual path

A Course in Miracles: Combined Volume (2008). Novato, California: Foundation for Inner Peace.

Bernstein, G. (2011), *Spirit Junkie: A Radical Road to Discovering Self-Love and Miracles*. London: Hay House UK.

Campbell, R. (2015), *Light is the New Black: A Guide to Answering Your Soul's Callings and Working Your Light*. London: Hay House UK.

Campbell, R. (2016), *Rise Sister Rise: A Guide to Unleashing the Wise, Wild Woman Within*. London: Hay House UK.

Cameron, J. (2016), *The Artist's Way: A Course in Discovering and Recovering Your Creative Self*. London: Macmillan.

Cohen, A. (2019), *Spirit Means Business: The Way to Prosper Wildly Without Selling Your Soul*. London: Hay House UK.

Dooley, M. (2014), *The Top Ten Things Dead People Want to Tell You*. London: Hay House.

Dyer, W. (2007), *Change Your Thoughts, Change Your Life: Living the Wisdom of the Tao*. London: Hay House UK.

Hay, L. and Holden, R. (2015), *Life Loves You: Seven Spiritual Practices to Heal Your Life*. London: Hay House UK.

Holden, R. (2013), *Loveability: Knowing How to Love and Be Loved*. London: Hay House UK.

Jeffers, S. (2007), *Feel the Fear and Do it Anyway: How to Turn Your Fear and Indecision into Confidence and Action*. London: Vermilion.

Williamson, M. (2015), *A Return to Love: Reflections on the Principles of 'A Course in Miracles'*. London: Harper Thorsons.

TUT **www.tut.com** To receive daily personalized messages from the Universe every day.

Meditation

Caddy, E. (2019), *Opening Doors Within: 365 Daily Meditations from Findhorn*. Inverness, Scotland: Findhorn Press.

Insight Timer – smartphone app offering guided meditations from some of the greatest teachers, plus meditation music and courses.

Any meditations by California-based meditation expert Davidji – find him on the Insight Timer app or at **www.davidji.com**

Diet and lifestyle for cancer survivors

Carr, K. (2008), *The Crazy Sexy Cancer Survivor: More Rebellion and Fire for Your Healing Journey*. Guildford, Connecticut: The Lyons Press.

Wark, C. (2018), *Chris Beat Cancer: A Comprehensive Plan for Healing Naturally*. London: Hay House UK.

ABOUT THE AUTHOR

Saskia Lightstar is a cancer misfit, a spiritual teacher, a wellbeing & happiness coach, an energy healer and an inspirational speaker. She screwed up everything in her life to get to where she is today; it took a lot of mistakes, failed businesses, divorces and being diagnosed with cancer, for her to find the willingness to venture down a spiritual path and become the happiest and greatest version of herself she has ever known.

Plagued by self-hate and low self-esteem for most of her life, Saskia has now become a happiness and self-love ninja, and guides others on how to be happier than they ever dreamt possible. She is a testament to the fact you can feel lost or 'less than' your whole life and still find your way to a place of confidence, happiness and peace.

Saskia is a proud misfit and non-conformist brimming with optimism and a joy that's contagious. She can usually be found roaming the forests of London with her French Bulldog, Barnaby Le French.

 @saskialightstar

 @saskia.lightstar

www.saskialightstar.com

HAY HOUSE

Look within

Join the conversation about latest products,
events, exclusive offers and more.

f Hay House

🐦 @HayHouseUK

📷 @hayhouseuk

♥ healyourlife.com

We'd love to hear from you!

CPSIA information can be obtained
at www.ICGtesting.com
Printed in the USA
LVHW110804010921
696586LV00003B/152